Toward an African Theology

Toward an African Theology

JOHN S. POBEE

Abingdon / Nashville

TOWARD AN AFRICAN THEOLOGY

Copyright © 1979 by Abingdon

Library of Congress Cataloging in Publication Data

POBEE, J S
    Toward an African theology.
    Bibliography: p.
    Includes index.
    1.   Theology, Doctrinal—Africa—History. 2.   Akans (African peo-
ple)—Religion. 3.   Black theology.   I.   Title.
    BT 30.A4P62   201'.1   78-21080

ISBN 0-687-42420-8

MANUFACTURED BY THE PARTHENON PRESS AT
NASHVILLE, TENNESSEE, UNITED STATES OF AMERICA

To
The Theological Education Fund (Third Mandate)
A Service of the Commission on the World Mission
and Evangelism of the World Council of Churches

Contents

Preface

The case for translating Christianity into authentic African categories hardly needs to be argued. That need has long been recognized in both Africa and Europe. It has been felt all the more since the wind of change that blew African countries into independent status. Unfortunately, most of the efforts so far have concentrated on criticizing the work of the early missionaries. I believe it is now time to be more positive and constructive than that. And this is the task I have set myself in this volume.

It has been my humble privilege to serve on the Committee of the Third Mandate of the Theological Education Fund, a Service of the Commission on World Mission and Evangelism of the World Council of Churches. This Committee has not only been funding theological education in the Third World but has also been exploring innovative patterns of theological education. It has endeavored to promote the contextualization of theology. The distinguished Executive Director of the Theological Education Fund, Dr. Shoki K. Coe, in an article in *Theological Education* (Autumn 1974) puts it thus: "By contextuality we mean wrestling with God's world in such a way as to discern the particularity of this historic moment; and by contextualization we mean the wrestling with God's word in such a way that the power of the incarnation which is the divine form of contextualization, can enable us to follow His steps to contextualize." The old adage is "the sweetness of the pudding is in the eating." Since our committee has been promoting contextualization, I thought I should do what our committee has been preaching. And so I come to write this volume entitled *Towards an African (Akan) Theology.* It is an attempt to hold a dialogue between the Christian faith and African tradition and custom in the flux and turmoil of our day. I dedicate this volume to the Third Mandate of the T.E.F., thus seeking to pay tribute not only to the T.E.F. as a committee but also to the director, Dr. Shoki Coe, and the associate directors: the Rev. Aharon Sapsezian, Dr. Ivy Choe, Dr. Jim A. Berquist, and the Rev. Mr. Desmond Tutu, who was the Associate Director of the Africa region of the T.E.F. until his elevation in 1975 to the Deanship of the Johannesburg Cathedral (the first time it had been filled by an African) and then again to the bishopric of Lesotho in 1976.

As luck would have it, I spent the academic year October 1974 to June 1975 as a fellow and a scholar in residence at the Institute for Ecumenical and Cultural Research at St. John's University, Collegeville, Minnesota. This manuscript was prepared at the Institute, although bits of it had already appeared in the *Ghana Bulletin of Theology.* I, therefore, wish to express my deepest gratitude to the institute for Ecumenical and Cultural Research for the invitation for the provision of excellent working conditions which made the 1974–1975 academic year a very fruitful year. And, of course, with that should go my gratitude to the University of Ghana for giving me a sabbatical leave from my University and to the Theological Education Fund for their financial contribution to my sojourn at the Institute.

Most of the chapters in this book were tried out at various institutions in the United States. It was my privilege to be guest lecturer at the University of North Carolina at Chapel Hill. Here I acknowledge my gratitude to Professors Charles Long and Arnold Nash for arranging the visit. Then I was also privileged to be guest lecturer to the Cluster of Theological Institutions, about nine of them and of mixed composition, in Chicago, Illinois. The lectures were given at the Auditorium of the Lutheran School of Theology in Chicago. Here I remember with special gratitude Professor James A. Scherer; the Professor of World Missions, Philip Hefner, instructor in the foundational course in the construction theology program;

and Adrienne Rooks and Shelby Rooks, the president of Chicago Theological Seminary. I am most grateful for these opportunities to try out these chapters as lectures. The discussions and comments were most invaluable.

I also recall with gratitude the opportunity to try out parts of it at the United Theological Seminary of the Twin Cities, New Brighton, Minnesota, and at the Lutheran Theological Seminary of St. Paul, Minnesota. At these two places I mention with gratitude Dr. Thomas Campbell, the academic vice-president of the former institute and my fellow worker on the Committee of the T.E.F., and Dr. Paul R. Sponheim, Dean of Academic Affairs at the latter institution.

I was also privileged to give some of these lectures at the Mennonite Theological Seminary at Elkhart, Indiana. Here Williard and Alice Roth, Robert Ramseyer, Paul Millar, C. J. Dyck, and David Shank had a lot to do with sharpening my thoughts on the subject.

Some of the lectures were also given at the United Theological College of the West Indies, Jamaica. Dr. and Mrs. Horace Russell and the staff were a great encouragement to me. Again, on my way back to Ghana from the Western Hemisphere, I was invited by the Northwestern Ordination Course to give some of these lectures at their summer school held in Manchester in August 1975. It was a great privilege and another source of inspiration. Here I recall with gratitude the Rev. Dr. Selby and the Rev. Patrick Vaughan.

There are several other subjects I would have liked to deal with in this volume, e.g., the absoluteness of Christ, the concept of God, and a number of ethical issues. It is my hope that I shall at a later stage continue the study in subsequent publications. But I am concerned to have a not-too-expensive volume and to encourage many, theologians and laymen alike, to read and address themselves to the subject. So I have chosen the path of brevity in this volume, but I have done a companion volume, not yet published, called *Aspects of Akan Religion.*

Finally, I acknowlege my indebtedness to Professor C. F. D. Moule, of the University of Cambridge; Dr. William Bilheimer, Director of the Institute for Ecumenical and Cultural Research; Professor Jerome Theisen, O.S.B., of St. John's University; the Rev. John Quinn, fellow and scholar-in-residence at the Institute; and the Rev. Dr. J. Christopher Thomas and Joshua N. Kudadjie, both my colleagues in the University of Ghana, for reading and commenting on parts of the manuscript. The Rt. Rev. John V. Taylor, Lord Bishop of Winchester, England, so kindly read the entire manuscript. Finally, I am deeply indebted to Mr. Joseph Nunoo for typing the manuscript for me. The final typing was done by Miss Evelyn Tetteh of the Office of the Dean of Arts at the University of Ghana. To her I owe great and deep gratitude.

J. S. Pobee

Toward an African Theology

I

Prolegomena

Christianity, originating in Palestine, came to Africa by a circuitous route. Of course, Christianity appeared in Egypt and Roman North Africa, not to mention Nubia, in the first three centuries of the church's existence, long before Western.Europe was Christianized. North African Christianity not only produced theological giants like Augustine of Hippo, Tertullian, and Cyprian, but also left indelible marks on Latin Christianity. Indeed, a good deal of what became Latin Christianity, or Christianity of the West, bears the marks of Augustine and Tertullian.

However, Christianity as it reached Africa south of the Sahara came via Europe and in recent times America. This observation is important because, since European powers like Britain, France, and Germany came to be colonial powers on the African continent, Christianity has often been charged with being an instrument employed by the European colonial powers to enslave and oppress the Africans. The late Kwame Nkrumah, the prince of African politics and nationalism in the fifties and sixties of the twentieth century, put it articulately and vividly:

> The stage opens with the appearance of missionaries and anthropologists, traders and concessionaires, and administrators. While the "missionaries" with "Christianity" implore the colonial

subject to lay up his "treasures in Heaven where neither moth nor rust doth corrupt," the traders and concessionaires and administrators acquire his mineral and land resources, destroy his arts, crafts and home industries.[1]

The message is clear: Christianity has been instrumental in the enslavement of *homo Africanus.*

Similarly the *Ghana Evening News* of March 26, 1960, carried a cartoon in which a bishop with a Bible in one hand hugged an expatriate soldier, with gun in hand, who had shot dead an African. The caption of the cartoon read: "Watch the Bible and not my action." The insinuation was that the bishop was an accomplice with European political power in the suppression of the native Africans.

The cartoon, like the statement of Mr. Nkrumah quoted earlier, expresses the allegation often made against the Christian church, namely that the church is an imperialist agent; that the colonial powers were consciously aided by the Christian missionary churches in the enslavement and suppression of Africans.

The examples cited are all examples of political enslavement. But the oppression extends also to the social sphere. Nii Akwaa Mensah II, Nai Wulomo (chief priest) of the Gă traditional area, said at a rally of the Convention Peoples Party:

> With the advent of Christianity and western civilisation we have been taught to disregard our way of living—a setback to our culture and an opportunity to the imperialists and their agents. . . . We have too much adopted the Christian way of life and if we could do as our forefathers did, there was no reason why we should not force the imperialists to go bag and baggage from our God-given land.[2]

These quotations are echoes, conscious or unconscious, of the Marxist charge against Christianity and all religion, that they are the opiate of the people.

Whether we agree with these statements is neither here nor there. The point remains indisputable that there is a feeling that Christianity has been an instrument of oppression in Africa. This is not unique of Africa. For blacks elsewhere have felt like this. Marcus Garvey, who founded the Universal Negro Improvement Association and created a scare in the Caribbean and North America early in this century, wrote on his concept of the Black God in these terms:

> If the white man has the idea of a white God, let him worship his God as he desires. If the yellow man's God is of his race let him worship his

God as he sees fit. We, as Negroes, have found a new idea. Whilst our God has no color, yet it is human to see everything through one's own spectacles, and since the white people have seen their God through white spectacles, we have only now started out (late though it be) to see our God through our own spectacles. The God of Isaac and the God of Jacob, let him exist for the race that believes in the God of Isaac and the God of Jacob. We Negroes believe in the God of Ethiopia, the everlasting God, God the Father, God the Son and God the Holy Ghost, the One God of all ages. That is the God in whom we believe, but we shall worship Him through the spectacles of Ethiopia.[3]

Of course, Garvey's concept of the Black God was intended as a rallying call to give dignity to the oppressed Negroes. But that apart, he stumbles onto a very important truth—the necessity to translate Christianity into Negro or African categories. For without that, Christianity will never be really integrated into African society. The simple truth is that Christianity, having reached Africa via Europe, came with a European stamp on it. And so in the African context, if there is to be a serious and deep communication and rooting of the gospel of Christ, the African stamp will have to replace the European stamp. My former teacher, the late Sidney G. Williamson, after a careful study of the appearance of Christianity among the Akan of the Gold Coast, otherwise known as Ghana, has rightly drawn the following conclusion:

> The Christian faith as historically implanted by western missionary enterprise among the Akan has proved unable to sympathize with or relate its message spiritually to Akan spiritual outlook. Its impact is thereby dulled. It has launched a frontal attack on Akan traditional beliefs and practices, and sought to emancipate the Akan from his traditional outlook. But the method and means adopted to secure this end, relying as they did on western enlightenment as set forth through a westernized form of Christianity, had the effect of calling the Akan out of his traditional environment, not of redeeming him within it. . . . The conviction that the Christian faith and Akan religion, encountering each other out of vastly different backgrounds and experience, view each other from a distance without common ground of fellowship, so that the impact never amounts to a real encounter, cannot be set aside.[4]

Our argument so far is that, in view of the rising political pressures like African nationalism and in order that the gospel may have real encounter with *homo Africanus*, there is need to translate Christianity into genuine African categories. This is what we call *African theology*. It is the attempt to couch essential Christianity into African categories and thought forms. Such an exercise is not to be confused with an exercise in couching African world view in Christian form. This means that there are certain aspects of the Christian faith which are *nonnegotiable*. For example, the cross of Christ is such a nonnegotiable tradition. To lose it is to lose the Christian message. We must first preach the gospel and allow it to bear fruit with the culture. And social activity, though also important in Christian witness, is not the first purpose of mission.

To announce the need for African theology is easy and reasonable. But it is far more difficult to construct it. Part of the trouble is the concept of *homo Africanus. Homo Africanus* is a multiheaded hydra, in much the same way as *homo sapiens* is a multiheaded hydra. In Africa there has been the impact of Westernism expressed through art, science, technology, learning, and social contact. In any case, as a result of Christianity becoming a part of European culture, African man after colonialism acquired laws, learning, art, and a concept of the state that was shaped by Christendom. Thus *homo Africanus* of 1976 is different from *homo Africanus* of 1876.[5] The communication and scientific revolution of our day means that even the most "primitive" African has advanced from his pristine stage to something else, precisely what we do not know. In other words, the question is, How indigenous is indigenous? How traditional is traditional? This warns against fossil culture and fossil religion. So when we use "African," we refer to the African people's religiousness in the flux and turmoil of the modern world. And that is no doubt rooted in the past. We wish to hold the past, present, and future together.

Again, there is a plethora of African cultures. Partly as a result of hard geographical and physical conditions, there is a gulf between Africa north of the Sahara and Africa south of the Sahara, between East Africa and West Africa. To confound the issue, within West Africa and even within the one country, like Ghana, there are remarkable differences based on tribal background. Thus the Akan groups of Ghana are by and large matrilineal, while the Ewe and the Ga groups of Ghana are patrilineal. Again in some tribes, e.g., the Akan of West Africa, the spirits of the ancestors are very important, while among others, e.g., the Masai of East Africa, they are no use. Thus the concept of "Africanness" is a very elusive one.

This fact of pluralism in society, not least in African society, appears to be part of the divine economy. First, the historical nature of revelation implies a pluralistic situation. Second, the whole theology of love operating through human life implies pluralism, because love can be accepted only freely and not by imposition. Freedom and the possibility of choice and variety go together. Third, the story of the Tower of Babel (Gen. 2:1-9) affirms pluralism as part of God's economy for the world.

Nevertheless, one would still maintain there is a sense in which an African is marked off from the Asian or the European or the American. There is a certain Africanness about the culture and religious beliefs and practices which can be so recognized. Only let us consciously find out how and to what extent African countries and African people have changed, lest we waste time preparing to evangelize the Africa of 1800, which no longer exists.

Even so, one would expect to find African theologies rather than one African theology which purports to speak to all conditions of *homo Africanus*. We make no apologies for pleading for African theologies because this is in fact how theology has been evolved over the years. After all, theology emerges from, among other things, a historic community and a people's experiences. Since these are diverse, there are bound to be diverse theologies. Thus in Europe and America we have within the same broad tradition pragmatists like Harvey Cox, scientific rationalists with a tinge of Heidegger like Rudolf Bultmann, "mystical a priori" like Paul Tillich, and even the post-religion man-come-of-age like Dietrich Bonhoeffer. These by no means exhaust the list.

The diversity makes the task all the more difficult. But it must be undertaken. Our aim is to communicate the Christian message to primarily the Akan of Ghana, although we also believe and trust it will be meaningful to many other groups in West Africa as a whole and to other citizens of the world outside Africa.

While we affirm a certain Africanness, we wish also to warn against treating African man as a museum piece or an anthropological curio. He has not been static; he has grown in stature, mentality, culture, and in other ways. But above all, he shares with the rest of mankind some human traits. In the ebb and flow of cultures, he has borrowed from other groups. Consequently, some of the things that may be paraded as African theology may yet speak to others

belonging to other racial groups. We see African theology as one
more fragment in the world mosaic of cultures and theologies.

In the next few paragraphs let us direct our attention to some
guidelines in the quest for African theology. First, since it is the
Christian faith that we wish to communicate in African terms, our
starting point should be the source of the church's faith. We refer to
the Bible, the foundation document of the church. African theology
has to be rooted in the Bible. We do not mean by this a literalistic
interpretation of it. Biblical criticism has to be taken seriously. In this
connection we also recommend the *religionsgeschichtliche Methode*.

> This method represents the most thorough-going application of a
> naturalistic historicism to the study of the Bible. It assumes that
> biblical religion, in both the Old and New Testaments passed
> through stages of growth and evolution like all ancient religions, and
> in this evolution was heavily influenced through interaction with its
> religious environment. This method involves the consistent
> application of the principle of analogy to biblical religion: the history
> and development of biblical religion must be analogous to the history
> and development of other ancient religions.[6]

There is one point of departure where we are concerned: whereas the
religionsgeschichtliche Methode refuses to be interested in the truth of
the Bible or in revelation, we as students of African theology should
be interested in the truth of the various revelations that confront us in
our situation. Besides, Christianity lays claim to a finality of
revelation. Thus by this method we shall be raising the fundamental
issue of the finality of Christ.

Still on the primary sources of the church's faith, we should take
serious notice of the tradition of the church. Tradition is not exactly
identical with church history. Tradition is the stream of apostolic life
and witness stretching from the apostles to all generations and areas,
though not immediately identifiable with them. It is the power of the
Holy Spirit, which gives life to the witness and mission of the
church. Whatever else we may say, it is important to start with the
Bible. For Christianity starts with God through Christ; the Christian
faith starts from what is given.

Such theology will have to be ecumenical. For too long, theology
has been denominational, partly because in the nineteenth century,
when serious mission in Africa was carried out, theologians and
churchmen took for granted that their denomination was the true
church. Consequently, the younger churches in Africa have been

cast as branches of European church organizations, manifesting post-Reformation theological and institutional categories. African theology must guard against white man's factionalism and be ecumenical. For in the true understanding of the church in the New Testament, unity and mission are inseparable, and that means co-operation and sharing of resources.

Second, our concern would also be with the revelation in African religion. On this we recommend the phenomenological approach. This is the analytical description originally pioneered by E. Husserl which was applied to theology.[7] The words of the late Paul Tillich are apposite here:

> Theology must apply the phenomenological approach to all its basic concepts, forcing its critics first of all to see what the criticized concepts mean and also forcing itself to make careful descriptions of its concepts and to use them with logical consistency, thus avoiding the danger of trying to fill in logical gaps with devotional material. The test of a phenomenological description is that the picture given by it is convincing, that it can be seen by anyone who is willing to look in the same direction, that the description illuminates other related ideas, and it makes the reality which these ideas are supposed to reflect understandable. Phenomenology is a way of pointing to phenomena as they "give themselves," without the interference of negative or positive prejudices and explanations.[8]

The phenomenological approach is recommended as the method for collecting the basic data of African religion. We as yet have no scriptures of African traditional religion. But the urgent task is the collection of myths, proverbs, invocations, prayers, incantations, ritual, songs, dreams, and so on. The collections made so far are rather haphazard and are part of sociological and anthropological studies. We are asking for the specifically theological mind to be brought to bear on the vast material of the sources of African traditional religion. It is in this study that the phenomenological approach is recommended as a method.

Of course, we are aware of weaknesses in the phenomenological approach. For example, it is difficult to know what is empirical, scientific study of religions through history. Again it fails to provide the criterion which should govern choice when one is confronted with contradictory revelations. It is silent on a rather important point in arguing for validity, i.e., where and when an idea was revealed. After using the phenomenological approach to lay bare the basic facts of the religion, we will go the extra mile to address ourselves to the issue of the truth and falsity of the religion.

Nevertheless, three advantages accrue from the phenomenological approach. First, since it begins with the phenomena themselves, the study begins at the right place, even if we do well also to bear in mind that everybody, even the most objective person, has presuppositions. Secondly, the approach is conducive to clarity in the sense that one knows what one is talking about, i.e., What is man? What is God? What is sin? and so on. Third, the phenomenological approach moves on a more secure ground because it proceeds by description rather than by deduction. That is, it does not start with *a priori* principles.

The third guideline—and this is the most difficult task—an effort should be made to confront the two views, not necessarily to make easy reconciliations, but to face their similarities and differences. At this stage, hermeneutics comes into its own—an attempt is made to understand the Word of God and how it is to be given to man in his own cultural milieu.

Finally, living as we do in an age of strife and conflict and impatience, we would urge that no good purpose is served by proceeding to vitriolic attacks on the earliest missionaries. In the long view of human development, blame in itself and excoriation after the event serve no useful and beneficial purpose because responsibility in any system is always delegated and can be diverted to someone else. Further, it is impossible, by and large, to accuse anyone of blatant insincerity and deliberate ungodliness. At the worst they can be castigated for their ignorance, timorousness, and stubbornness. But that does not solve the problem and the task of building up an African theology. The task can be undertaken without bitterness.

African theology is concerned to interpret essential Christian faith in authentic African language in the flux and turmoil of our time so that there may be genuine dialogue between the Christian faith and African cultures. This, though in the first instance an intellectual activity, is a handmaid of the mission of the church. African theology should be the handmaid of worship of Christ by the church, both in its narrow cultic sense and in its broad sense of Christian living. African theology should never be an end in itself; it should serve the cause of clarity of faith and worship in our specific African and human context which is one manifestation of the universal human experience.

Ideally, African theologies should be in the vernacular. Language is more than syntax and morphology; it is a vehicle for assuming the weight of a culture. Therefore, this attempt to construct an African theology in the English language is the second best, even if it is convenient if it should secure as wide a circulation as possible.

II

From Theology to African Theology

The Copernician revolution has dislodged man from the center of life and stripped him of his privileges.[1] The new dimensions of astrophysics seem to dwarf man into insignificance. Evolution has stressed the apparent insignificance of man in the universe. Further, it has taught man that the universe is a self-regulating mechanism. It accordingly tends to exorcise the universe of the supernatural. This puts a question mark against the place and relevance of theology in society today.

Again, even within the Christian church there are committed and serious Christians, including some clergymen, who distrust theologians and have serious misgivings about the discipline called theology. Their information is that theology undermines faith and is accordingly, suspect. Many have been treated to the apocryphal story that at a road junction there stood a sign which read: "Left to faith and Heaven, Right to theology lecture-room and Hell." It is then alleged that the theologians took the latter road. The story makes theology and faith alternatives and castigates theology for lack of true religion and faith.

The burden of our argument so far is that one of the challenges of the twentieth century is theological. Taking the example of Christianity, the challenge may be put in a series of questions: What is Christianity? Is it true? How does it help life and satisfy the human predicament? Why must the church's teaching and pronouncements with regard to wealth or sex be preferable to what other groups in society are saying on the subject? With the urgent population problem threatening the well-being of man, what hearing should be given to the pope, who speaks for millions all over the world in protest against artificial birth control? What hearing is to be given to Christians on bioethics, on eugenics, on genetic medicine? These are some of the burning issues of our time. Some of these questions may be raised of other religions. Truly, the challenge of theology for our time is unavoidable. "A wit has said *homo sapiens* can be distinguished from the other primates by the fact that whenever two or three of them are gathered together, there you will find theological argument and fermented liquor."[2] There may be argument over fermented liquor, but there can be no serious and fundamental objection to the unavoidability of theological discussion. For man has the inveterate habit of wondering about himself and his existence. And that is what theology is *inter alia* concerned with.

Three more arguments confirm us in our convictions about the unavoidability of theology. First, religion is one aspect of human existence, standing alongside other areas like politics, economics, and society. If man is to have a balanced view of life and be able to live a full life, he must make provision for the study of each of the constituent aspects of human existence. Theology is concerned with the religious aspect of these items. Therefore, it still has a place in man's education. Theology must be given a place in every educational curriculum because

> in an age in which translations of the Bible and the Christian classics circulate in paperbacks by the hundreds of thousands it would indeed be philistine irresponsibility to deny undergraduates the opportunity of studying the history of religious thought at a properly academic level. If an important object of humane studies is to understand how we have come to think and believe as we do, it would be stultifying to omit all reference to a part of our tradition which has so largely shaped our language, or ideas, our laws, our institutions and perhaps even something still carried over into our behavior.[3]

These words were written of Christian theology. To his references to the Bible, we would add the Koran, Buddhist scriptures, and others. To understand the civilizations of the East and Near East, we must study the religious elements which have so shaped those civilizations.

A second consideration is a fact amply demonstrated by sociological and anthropological studies, namely that African traditional life from which our studies should start and with which all our studies should be concerned, if they are to have any relevance and meaning, "is intensely and pervasively religious."[4] Any outline of the culture of any ethnic group unavoidably involves a discussion of their religion.[5] It is difficult to distinguish sharply between the religious and the nonreligious, between the sacred and secular. In African societies, religion stares people in the face at all points—at birth, at puberty, at marriage, at death, and at national or tribal festivals. Thus religion is as vocal as it is dynamic in African society and cannot be meaningfully sidestepped. Theology has a place, and rightly so, and must be on the curriculum.

The third consideration is the link between religion and morality. Religion is, among other things, concerned with ethics or morality. It is even claimed that religion and morality are inseparable. Christianity, for example, makes this affirmation, as is evidenced by James 1:27: "The kind of religion without stain or fault in the sight of God our Father is this: to go to the help of orphans and widows in their distress and keep oneself untarnished by the world" (NEB). True religion requires a person to show deep and genuine concern for the well-being of others. There are several other passages from the Bible which make this point—the parable of the sheep and goats in Matthew 25; Romans 12; I John 4:20-21; and others.

Similarly, the concept of *saman yarba* among the Akan of Ghana makes the point that religion and morality, theology and ethics are inseparable. The phrase literally means disease caused by a ghost or the spirit of the ancestors who surround the living and on whose good will the living depend for their well-being. The idea is that a ghost can afflict with disease a living being who does not contribute to the well-being of the society. The lesson is that to avoid *saman yarba* a man must avoid evils which will outrage the spirit-beings. And that fear of *saman yarba* is "encased" in religion. It is easy to dismiss such ideas as unnecessary and untrue. We refuse to indulge in such discussion because it is idle talk. Our conviction is that no serious and solid development is possible unless it is pitched at the wavelength of the people or, if you like, the psychology of the addressees. As the psychologist C. G. Jung once wrote: "If something which seems to me an error shows itself to be more effective than a truth, then I must first follow up the error, for in it lie power and life which I lose if I hold to what appears to me true." So since religion and moral choices pervade society and life, they cannot be meaningfully ignored; or rather, they may be ignored to one's own peril. Let me hasten to add to the quotation from Jung that I do not believe religion to be "error."

We may at this point throw in another argument, which we shall not argue. We beieve that in an age desperately searching for liberty, religion has a lot to contribute. As Lactantius perceptively put it: "It is in religion alone that liberty dwells. . . . No one can be made to adore what he does not wish."[6] Theology has this lesson of liberty to teach to the world.

It is now time to define theology, even though the discussion so far has assumed that it has to do with religion. But let us first dismiss certain erroneous views about the discipline, or say what theology is not.

Theology is not abstruse speculation, an academic game, running the danger of raising and answering questions which no one asks. For example, medieval theologians wrote theses on how many angels could dance at the tip of a needle. Such abstruse speculation is not of the essence of theology. Again, there has been the danger of overdefinition. For example, Nestorius' objections to the description of Mary as "*Theotokos*" may be viewed in the light of overdefinition.[7] That danger is also in part a legacy of the Latin legal tradition and inheritance of the West. There is also the danger of overintellectualization. Excesses of any form are wrong. Finally, there is the danger for theologians to behave like God's private secretaries, talking as if we had all the answers. Certainly Christianity claims that God cannot be fathomed in his totality: "O the depth of the riches of the wisdom and knowledge of God! How unsearchable are his judgments and inscrutable his ways!" (Rom. 11:33 RSV). And, therefore, "we walk by faith, not by sight" (II Cor. 5:7 RSV). There can, therefore, be no place for overconfidence or cocksureness. However, these and other such aberrations should not be confused with genuine and authentic theology. Abuse does not do away with true use. Our concern in indicating abuses of theology is to ensure that nothing in creation, not even theology, separates us from God. And the genius of the Christian religion is that it has always managed to survive its distortions.

Professor J. Macquarrie has defined theology as "the study which, through participation in and reflection upon a religious faith, seeks to express the content of the faith in the clearest and most coherent language available."[8] This definition is questionable because it is too static, not sufficiently allowing for the process element in all religions. The definition takes as its starting point a corpus of doctrines and practices and studies how that corpus can be communicated in another culture or faith.

However, in our opinion, Christian theology should be concerned with a gospel and not a religion. The starting point should be the "Christ event," the scientific identification of which is the task of theology. Further, theology should reflect on the implications of that Christ event for those who see the world in a particular way. Theology should discover what that Christ event looks like when seen from within that particular world view. Thus to some degree theology is always being written by those to whom the gospel is being communicated. Furthermore, it is the task of theology to keep on reconstructing and repairing a holistic Christocentric world view, a synthesis of the knowledge which is being expounded by analytical departmentalized study, to help people to relate their own understanding and interests to a comprehensive whole.

Five elements may be identified in theology. First, it presupposes a *faith*, i.e, the beliefs and practices deriving therefrom of a people in connection with the supranatural, in connection with the meaning and purpose of life. Theology presupposes the convictions of a people with regard to the meaning and purpose of life and human existence. A man may look at the moon and the stars, the rhythm and order in the created world and come to the conclusion that "the heavens declare the glory of God; and the firmament sheweth his handiwork" (Ps. 19:1). Whether such an interpretation of the phenomena of nature is valid is not our concern here. Our concern is that this is one conviction of some people.

Similarly, a traditional Ghanaian, be he Akan, Ewe, Gă, or whatever, believes he is surrounded by numerous hosts of spirit-beings, some good, some evil, who are able to influence the course of his life for good or for ill. So he believes in the Supreme Being, gods, and ancestors, and tries to get their goodwill in all sorts of ways. The practices and religious exercises dramatize this belief of the traditional Ghanaian.

Faith itself is made possible by *revelation*. There is no time here for a lengthy discourse of revelation. But by it we understand the initiative of that to which faith is directed.[9] As Macquarrie puts it, "The quest for the sense of existence is met by the gift of a sense of existence."[10] It is the cognitive element in experience, and there are various ways of experiencing it. The very existence of different religions, all of which claim to be the way to Divinity, is itself proof conclusive of the various ways of experiencing revelation. It need not always be traumatic and it may be mediated through ordinary events of everyday life. Indeed, history is the arena of God's confrontation with man. So a sense of history should be important in our understanding of revelation.

It is also important to remember that faith is the faith of a historical community. Christianity, for example, was born in the matrix of Judaism and in a Semitic context. It began as a conviction of a people from a particular background. Similarly, Islam originated from the historical setting of Arabia. Thus it can be demonstrated that the strict monotheism of Islam and its uncompromising attitude to idolatry is in part the reaction to the polytheism and polydaemonism of Arabia at the time.[11]

The importance of faith being the faith of a historic community cannot be labored more. It means faith speaks from a specific faith. A theology that is valid in a particular context must come out of that context of experience.

An essential element in the study of the faith of a community is *reflection*. In other words, faith though it be, it must be subjected to thought, to a critical, descriptive, and interpretative analysis. Earlier on, attention was drawn to the tendency in some quarters to contrast faith and reason, faith and theology. If religion is one aspect of a person's personality, then he is obliged to use his reason, which is a part of his personality, when he addresses himself to religion. Faith implies the commitment of the whole person in all his faculties, thinking, feeling, and willing. Thus reflection on that faith is an essential element of theology. Christian theology, therefore, must be an articulate system of thought interpreting what is implied in the faith of Christ. Similarly, Islamic theology will be an articulate system of thought interpreting what is implied in the faith of Mohammed. Despite the claim by earlier scholars that African traditional religion is danced out, not thought out, even African traditional religion involves reflection on the beliefs of a people.[12] When a man throws down his first morsel of food, it cannot be a thoughtless waste of food. He reasons that he is "buying" the goodwill of the numerous hosts of spirits around him, who influence his life for good or for ill. Or again, when an illness is diagnosed by a traditionalist as the result of the evil eye of the witch in the family, reflection upon the experience of a man in the world has already taken place.

It is easy to announce the need for reflection. But that immediately raises the problem of technique. It is bound to be linguistic, if it is true that language is the soul of a people. Language is a vehicle for assuming a culture, to support the weight of a civilization. It helps to shape one's relationship to reality. Our language is imposed on us by the particular social group in which we are socialized from earliest days. Through it we interpret and define our existence and therefore our values.

We are not asking to be overburdened with linguistic study. Two examples should suffice, one from Akan society, the other from Christianity. Authentic Akan society never says "the chief is dead." For against the background of the concept of sacral kingship, the chief never dies; rather he is gathered to his forebears. So the normal way of announcing the death of a chief is to say "the chief has gone to the village." A literal understanding of the sentence just laid out above will be far from the idea it is intended to convey. Therefore, adequate knowledge of the language is a necessary tool.

Another example is taken from the *Book of Common Prayer* of the Anglicans. In it stands the following prayer: "Prevent us, O Lord, in all our doings, with thy most gracious favour, and further us with thy continual help; that in all our works begun, continued and ended in thee, we may glorify thy holy name, and finally by thy mercy obtain everlasting life; through Jesus Christ our Lord, Amen." Our concern is with the word "prevent." Today it means to stop or hinder. This meaning is far from the original meaning of the word. It meant "to go before as a guide" (cf. Latin *praevenire*). So once more a linguistic study is a necessary tool and unavoidable. And it is imperative to do this because if any converts are to be made, it is important and necessary to reinterpret the old language into contemporary language, and that is possible only when we have penetrated the original language.

Again, reflection should involve a textual study. In this area it is relatively easier to deal with the world religions, because those faiths have been codified in the first instance in a book or books. Thus

Christians have their Bible; Muslims have the Koran; Buddhists and the Hindus have their scriptures.[13] These texts come from particular milieus and reflect specific world views. Therefore, a textual study is necessary. For example, the Bible presupposes the cosmogony of a three-decker universe: an earth on which we live, a heaven above it, and Sheol underneath the earth. Modern scientific man is challenging the notion of heaven above or "out there," because he claims it is all space, through which Yuri Gagarin, John Glenn, and others have traveled and saw not even the skirts of the garment of God. Do we then simply scrap the notion of heaven? Whatever we do with the notion of heaven, the scientific academic must in the interest of science and fairness, allow the text to make its claims articulately and meaningfully in its context before it is rejected or reinstated. And this cannot be thoroughly achieved without a study of the text.

The issue of textual study as it relates to primal religions is a very tricky one because they were not originally "religions of the book," nor do they as yet have serious collections of their text. As was said in the first chapter, this is the urgent task for African theology. When the texts are collected, then comes the interpretation of the texts.

The reflection also has to be archaeological. If the light thrown on ideas in Judaism, Christianity, and Islam by archaeological discoveries is any guide, African religions will benefit immensely from archaeological studies relating to African religions and culture. Certainly archaeological studies in Egypt, for example, have told us a lot about the people's beliefs about death and afterlife. It is our submission that the archaeological approach to African religions is only now beginning, if not yet to begin.[14]

In the last several paragraphs, the argument has been that because revelation is mediated through historical events and historical persons, the revelation must be subjected to intelligent judgments in its historical, literary, textual, and philological aspects, in the light of all the available evidence.

Now we turn to another important element in theology, namely participation. The theologian, unlike the philosopher of religion who is very detached, is the spokesman of a religious community. Despite the prerequisite of objectivity, theology as well implies participation.

In the past, the tendency was to run down faiths other than one's own. Thus the Muslim was unfortunately looked upon by the

Christians at the time of the Crusades as the infidel. The motto of
Prince Henry the Navigator of Portugal (1395–1460) was *"infideles
debent subjuci fidelibus."* Needless to say by *"infideles"* he meant the
Muslims, who had made life precarious for Christian Europe.
Similarly, African traditional religion was all too often stigmatized as
the work of Satan and contemptuously described as fetishism.[15] All
these are examples of the militancy and exaggerated claims that
characterized evangelism and theology at one stage in the church's
history. Today we are doing better than before, thanks in part to the
phenomenological approach.

Finally, theology seeks to summarize a faith. It is an intellectual
discipline in the sense that it is marked by intelligibility and
consistency. The point of all the linguistic, textual, and
archaeological discipline is to bring intelligibility and coherence and
consistency into the faith.

Our efforts so far have been devoted to highlighting the main
elements in theology. Let us now turn to formative factors in
theology: (a) experience, (b) revelation, (c) scripture, (d) tradition, (e)
culture, (f) reason. Again, here we can only be sketchy.

Revelation means the disclosure of divinity to man in acts, in
deeds, and in historical events. It is the primary source of faith
because religion is, by and large, as much a man's search for God as
a man's response to God's self-disclosure. The response takes diverse
forms, sometimes gross, sometimes highly developed, sometimes
full of errors. Indeed, the distinction between special and general
revelation is worth recall. For the present, let us dwell on general
revelation. The Bible, for example, does not deny that the Gentile
has some revelation of God. But his plight is that he has actually
confused the revelation about the creature with the revelation about
the Creator (Rom. 1:19-20). "Paul is serious in affirming that natural
man has a knowledge of God, and he represents this natural human
knowledge of God as the effect of the special purpose of God. It is not
adequate to say that God is known as an object is known which
remains passive as man examines and comes to know it. God is
known because He makes Himself known."[16]

Next door to revelation are *scripture* and *tradition*. The world
religions have their scriptures, which codify their traditions. The
traditions arose in historical circumstances. Scripture and tradition
are culture-ridden. To that extent, the scriptures are historical and
should be thus studied. But at the same time, these scriptures are

considered revelatory of divine activity. Theology must have scriptures as a plumbline. Christianity, for example, is a faith that is based on a completely definitive revelation for the world and cannot be superseded by something else.

Apart from the scriptures, there are other traditions which did not get into the canon of scriptures. These are helpful, as well as commentaries or earliest understandings of the faith of the particular religion. So they are bound to be illuminating in one way or other. There is one problem with regard to tradition. Churches are divided over the use of tradition. For example, whereas Anglicans make use of the Church Fathers up to the end of the fifth century, Roman Catholics go beyond the fifth century to the Lateran Councils and even beyond. Others do not welcome even the first five centuries. For ourselves we seek to be flexible and examine each tradition in the light of the biblical faith and its spirit.

Once revelation and scriptures are mentioned, opponents of religion have sometimes argued as though faith and *reason* are alternatives. Faith is demanded of man—heart, soul, and body. Therefore, he must come to faith with his reason, among other things. Insofar as revelation has been mediated through historical processes, one must approach the revelation by asking intelligent questions, whether historical, literary, textual, or philological, in the light of the available evidence. So reason is a must in theology.[17]

Now we return to the issue of theology and experience. Theology is rooted in, among other things, man's experiences or a people's experiences. This point is well demonstrated by the conflict between Augustine of Hippo and Pelagius, a British monk who lived in the fourth century A.D. Augustine had been a riotous man in his early life. He had had to struggle with several ideologies and philosophies before he settled for Christianity. In his own life and experience, much as he wanted to leave behind his licentious way of life, he still prayed, "Give me continence, O Lord, but not yet." Indeed, the soul was willing, but the flesh was weak. Consequently, he came to hold that only God's grace could deliver him from his dilemma. His experience became the paradigm for all men. The result of his historical experiences was that his theology hinged on the doctrine of grace, i.e., the unmerited favor of God toward men. Hence Augustine came to earn the title *doctor gratiae*. On the other hand, Pelagius, who had been a pious recluse of a monastic, could not leave everything to grace but sought to emphasize works or human effort. Pelagius himself had been a man of high moral character and fiber, and was consequently shocked by the low moral standing and state of the city of Rome around A.D. 400. Consequently, he rejected or at least played down the doctrine of original sin, which seemed to him to give men an easy escape from blame by attributing the universal proneness to sin to a vitiated nature inherited from Adam, the first man. His line of approach was that every man must brace up and master the powers of evil. Our concern here is not to adjudicate in the dispute between Augustine, on the one hand, and Pelagius, on the other hand. Our concern is to show that one's experiences to some extent determine one's theology.[18]

In our day, the most striking example is the emergence of black theology, in America and South Africa. The description of theology as "black" may sound odd, as much as to speak of "white" or "yellow" or "red" theology would sound odd. However, one can accept the description "black theology." "Black" may be used in either of two ways: (a) a literal sense—black in color; in this sense it is one of the five that comprise the mosaic, namely black, white, yellow, brown, red; (b) black as the symbol of something. And what is that something?

In America, as in South Africa, "black" is associated with poverty, ignorance, misery, terror, and insult. It contrasts with "white," the symbol of lords and masters of history and the gospel, the automatic heirs of the chief seats in the great parliament of humanity. To be black concretely means to be poor, to die of hunger, to be illiterate, to be exploited by others, to be treated as though you are not a person, and, sadly enough, sometimes not to know that you are a person—in short to live a subhuman existence. The black man finds himself relegated to the limbo of mankind.[19] Black is the symbol of evil, sin, wretchedness, death, war, famine, bad luck, and ugliness, i.e., it stands in contrast to white, the symbol of justice, truth, virginity, and beauty. I believe it is in this latter sense that "black" appears as an epithet of theology in the phrase "black theology." It is the theological reflection that springs from the experience of people of black pigmentation, who are discriminated against or oppressed in diverse manners by "whites" as the symbol of the sum total of power within the universe of black experience. Consequently, black theology appears to be primarily a theology of liberation from diverse manifestations of oppression. Black theology is born out of the black experience and is a theology of liberation, bringing good news to the poor in spirit and freedom to the oppressed. As James H. Cone, the archpriest of black theology, puts it, the blackness of God and everything implied by the phrase in a racist society is the heart of black theology's doctrine of God.[20] Thus black theology is to be seen as part of the whole black self-concept movement, which has for its motto, so to speak, "Black is beautiful". And so Deotis Roberts has written "Revelation to the blackman is a revelation of Black Power, which includes black awareness, black pride, black self-respect and a desire to determine one's own destiny."[21]

Just to make the record more complete, let us add a note on the black self-concept movement. That movement has been manifested in diverse ways: as a fiery summer at Watts, Newark, and Detroit in 1967. That is often remembered and tends to mislead observers into believing that the black self-concept movement is of necessity a violent one. However, violence is not of the essence of it, as other manifestations amply demonstrate. Thus there has been the approach of nonviolence, the archpriest of which was the late Dr. Martin Luther King, Jr.[22] Enhancing the black self-concept is still going on through literature produced by young black writers like Don Lee, Sonja Sanchez, and Carolyn Rodgers, through the use of rock or pop songs, poetry, visual arts, dance, and so on.[23] "That search for the definition of the black heritage is a search that begins inevitably with the black Church, for the black Church is the mother of the black experience in America."[24]

Christianity has been misused throughout its long history. It has sometimes been an instrument in the enslavement of one section of society or other. Thus W. H. Grier and P. M. Cobbs depicted Christianity as an enslaving force and the paragon of bigotry.[25] Consequently, they prefer "black morality" or the capacity for greatness. By that they mean, the blacks "have taken a Jesus Bag shaped like a noose and refashioned it into a black cornucopia of spiritual riches." One accepts the point about the misuse of Christianity. But one would insist that abuse does not do away with true use. It is not of the essence of Christianity to preach superiority of whites to blacks. To preach that is to corrupt authentic Christianity, which insists that "in Christ there is neither Jew nor Greek, bond nor free, but all are one." In any case, in Black Africa, Christianity demonstrably has been the "guardian angel of African nationalism."

As has been said above, the keynote of black theology is liberation with special reference to racist oppression. If, as we believe, the Word of God comes to man not *in vacuo* but in his concrete situations, reaching men in the depths of their personal lives, then black theology is a legitimate pursuit. However, there is one comment we shall venture, not necessarily in criticism but as an invidious and insidious danger to be watched. There is the danger of stopping at retaliation in the pursuit of liberation in a racist society. There is the danger of an apostle of liberation being enslaved by the idea of liberation. So there is need for a constant reminder that in the Christian view, liberation should go with reconciliation. For as Paul puts it at II Corinthians 5:17-19: "If anyone is in Christ, he is a new creation; the old has passed away, behold, the new has come. All this is from God, who through Christ reconciled us to himself and gave us the ministry of reconciliation; that is, in Christ God was reconciling the world to himself, not counting their trespasses against them, an entrusting to us the message of reconciliation" (RSV; cf. Eph. 2:14). That theme is a nonnegotiable element of the Christian faith. Thus bitterness and vindictiveness should have no place in black theology that is truly Christian.

The message of reconciliation is urgent and vital in this twentieth century which has experienced too many national enmities and varieties of nationalism: there have been Breton, Walloon, Welsh, Basque, African nationalisms. There has been mutual hatred leading to the extermination of whole peoples, as in the Nigerian Civil War. There has been racial strife in Russia, in South Africa, in the United States. Consequently, the call for reconciliation has been described as unrealistic and even misguided. In February 1975 Dr. Shelby Rooks invited me to take his class on black theology. In the discussion following my presentation, a number of American blacks, aged between twenty and thirty years, emphasized to me the lack of realism in preaching reconciliation. One of them so vividly put it thus: "The plea for reconciliation was preached before Shelby's time and we are in 1975 still talking of it and to no effect. So we are barking up the wrong tree."

Alongside that approach, we have also the proclamations of the apostles of hate and segregation, typified by the early Black Muslims and the early Malcolm X, also known as Malcolm Little and El-Hajj Malik El-Shabazz. For example, Elijah Muhammed, founder of the Black Muslims of the U.S.A. wrote: "It is impossible for Negroes and Whites to live together. I hate the few drops of white blood that is already in me. There is no intelligent black man who wants integration."[26] To them, integration is impossible because of the realities of the power situation: it is possible for blacks and whites to walk together as brothers and equals only when blacks too have a position of strength.

For ourselves the proclamations of the prophets of hate are counsels of despair even if we acknowledge the need for political strength. For one thing, hate is ultimately self-defeating because it sooner or later reduces one to the very wicked acts which one condemned in his oppressors. For another thing, hate is difficult to sustain forever, even if it may be useful at one point or other. While hate in blacks, and for that matter any oppressed groups, may serve the useful purpose of indicating to the whites what the blacks were thinking and that the blacks were critical and bitter, yet one still is haunted by the question, How long can the hate be sustained? In this connection it is not without significance that both Elijah Muhammad and Malcolm X modified their positions with time. Yet another reason is that no group, not even the oppressed, is flawlessly righteous and without its share of inhumanity, injustice, and arrogance. It takes two to make a war, and we have to be careful about self-righteousness. Complacency cannot purge anyone of guilt.

So we opt for integration, which is an expression of the biblical idea of reconciliation. We reject the attitude called by Andrei D. Sakharov "empirical competitive"—i.e., "a method aimed at maximum improvement of one's position everywhere possible and, simultaneously, a method of causing maximum unpleasantness to opposing forces without consideration of common welfare and common interests."[27] For that reduces politics to gambling and leads, at the best, to a dead end. On the other hand, neither can we accept false detente, collusion-detente, and capitulation-detente, because these are bogeys and devilish parodies of true reconciliation.

By reconciliation we mean rapprochement of peoples, individuals, and nations alike. Of course, there is a real problem about the pursuit of rapprochement without the democratization of the oppressive system. Rapprochement without the democratization of the oppressive system amounts to the acceptance of the rules of the game laid down by the oppressor; it amounts to capitulation in the face of oppressive power. It enables the oppressor to bypass problems which he cannot resolve on his own and makes it possible for him to concentrate on accumulating further strength. Rapprochement must be associated with the simultaneous elimination of the oppressor's isolation. [28] Reconciliation means integration, which means more than just social intermingling between blacks and whites, oppressed and oppressor, the poor and the rich. It also means the situation in the society should be equalized more than it is now. It means different people living together without losing their individuality and complexity; it means renouncing engrained prejudices and what Dostoevsky has called "shortcuts to thought." True integration eschews hatred and mutual recrimination; it means eschewing a preoccupation with calculating one another's guilt. It means mutual trust, open society, free dissemination of information, respect for the fundamental rights of the individual—black or white, democratization, respect for every person's right to choose where he wishes to live, and so on.

At this point a word about church unity as one important area of reconciliation is not out of place. The divisions of the church are a scandal. The credibility of a church which claims to have a ministry of reconciliation gets lost when she is so hopelessly divided and the members are at each other's throats. Therefore, to our mind, reconciliation must begin with the household of faith if our ministry of reconciliation is to carry conviction.

Black theology and African theology are related but not synonymous. They are related insofar as black Americans originated from Africa, and consequently share similarities. They are related also in this that Africans have been discriminated against and raped by colonialism. Consequently, black Africans and black Americans have this in common, that they have been the underprivileged and disinherited of the earth.

However, there are striking and perceptible differences between the circumstances of the American blacks and most of black Africa. For one thing, although American blacks have tended to romanticize Africa, stressing common genetic and historical cultural roots, their knowledge of Africa is clouded by generations of separation and years of brain-washing. Time did not stop in Africa when Africans were shipped from Africa across the Atlantic to the Western hemisphere. The social and cultural landscape has been radically altered. American blacks and African blacks differ because the former have been unable to retain the most important structural, uniting institutions through which the sense of social identity might have been retained by individuals. We refer to such things as the tribe, the council of elders, and so forth. African cultural institutions have been lost through loss of oral literature, recounting ancient authors and language. Furthermore, the experiences of American blacks are very different from the experiences of black Africa. For with the exception of the Republic of South Africa and Southern Rhodesia, racial prejudice is not as bad in Africa as in America. At least most of the African countries are today self-governing. Consequently, African theology, though interested in liberation, is not preoccupied with liberation from racial oppression as much as black theology is. The concern of African theology is to attempt to use African concepts and African ethos as vehicles for the communication of the gospel in an African context.

There is one more point of similarity and yet a difference. Religion is an integral part of the experience of blacks whether in America or black Africa. One can think of the Negro spirituals, folklore, art, sermons, literature, and history of American blacks. The case for black Africa hardly needs to be argued. But precisely at this point of agreement we see a marked difference. The one single greatest religious influence among American blacks is Christianity. George Washington once said: "True religion affords government its surest support."[29] Abraham Lincoln also said: "The only assurance of our nation's safety is to lay our foundation in morality and religion." The point of both quotations is that religion, by which they mean the Christian religion, is the substratum of American beliefs and ways. And indeed, America was born in the cradle of a powerful Christian spiritual revival. The Great Awakening of 1740 filled the colonists with the desire for human freedom, leading to the founding of a free nation. The great name was George Whitefield, a twenty-five-year-old British evangelist who preached far and wide in America that man should and could be born again through God's Spirit and that freedom is for every man in Jesus Christ. Several of the enlightened economic principles of the new nation were shaped by the revival in England, pioneered by John Wesley—for example, the elimination of oppressive labor practices and the free labor movement. And down the decades, America has been confronted—nay, challenged—by such evangelical giants as D. L. Moody, Martin Luther King, Jr., and Billy Graham who awakened the conscience of America. But in Africa there are diverse influences—African traditional religions, which are hardly known in black

America; Christianity; and Islam, which is hardly a first-order experience of the American blacks. Thus African theology has to contend with more religions than black theology. And this brings us to the last formative factor of theology, namely culture, because the use of "African" as an epithet of theology is also along cultural lines.

Culture refers to "all the modes of thought and behaviour, all the experiences, the entire social heritage which are handed down from one generation to another through communication, interaction and learning."[30] It covers political, economic, kinship, educational, and religious institutions of a people. One suspects that the differences between various religions of the world is, in part at any rate, the result of cultural differences. For after all, a person normally speaks out of his own being and experience. And being and experience are part of one's culture. Theology will be an anachronistic irrelevance unless it is pitched at the wavelength of the addressee as a person, in his ideologies, moods, and needs. It is difficult for one to know whither he is going, if he does not know whence he is coming. Consciousness of oneself guarantees communication. And for all the several problems, it is necessary to pass through a national phase to achieve an international consciousness.

Acknowledging the need for African theology is easy, but it is only the beginning of the study and of problems. The fundamental problem is, What is man? Who is *homo sapiens?* Who is *homo Africanus?* There is no prototype, as we argued in an earlier chapter. Thus we can only expect African theologies rather than an African theology. In any case, the experience of the world of scholarship and of believers is that no one formulation of theology speaks or can speak to all men, or even to all Christians for that matter. Few there be who can master all these approaches and be able to speak from and to them. The difficulty should warn against theological sloganeering because one cannot find a universally comprehensible theology. It should warn against arrogance and overconfidence.

We are lucky that anthropologists and sociologists like R. S. Rattray, K. A. Busia, E. Meyerowtiz, E. Pritchard, and others have collected for us the world views of various ethnic groups in Africa. What is needed now is an examination of the major ideas of any religion against the indigenous background. For example, what statement about Christ can be made when his person and work are seen and reflected upon from within an African culture?

At this point let us risk being charged with being repetitive. In the translation of Christianity into African categories, we must be on our guard against frivolous translations. The historic churches in Ghana, and for that matter most of Africa, have translated European hymns into the vernacular and suppose that they have thus indigenized Christianity. To us this is frivolous because the translations have become musical nonsense. The point is, you cannot force African words into European verse meters and get good results. Besides, the imageries in these hymns are so foreign that they make little impact. Fancy singing "In the bleak mid-winter" on a hot African evening—most of the singers would not have seen snow or winter, nor could they imagine it.

Again, we will iterate that no living language is static. We illustrated this point earlier with the change in meaning of the word "prevent." The danger in the use of the vernacular is the tendency to want to use old "classical" forms which are hardly ever used in contemporary society. For example, one translation of Matthew's Gospel into Fanti renders Matthew 2:2—"Where is he who as been born king of the Jews? For we have seen his star in the East, and have come to worship him" (RSV)—in the following manner: "*Abofra a woawo no Jewfo hen no wɔ hen? Ber a no woraba puee boka no, yehunii, na yeaba dɛ yerobokotow no.*" My query about this perfectly classical translation concerns the last clause, "have come to worship him," which is in Fanti "*yerobokotow no.*" The latter expression in modern usage has unpleasant associations. For example, it may be used to describe a man during a soccer match stooping under an opponent so as to give him a nasty fall. Or, at the best, the verb "*kotow*" followed by an object means to entreat, which is far from what the Greek word προσκυνησαι means.

Finally, theology as it faces culture must avoid anxious apology. For

> an anxious apologist is a contradiction in terms, and the very assertiveness aroused by the concern to preserve tends all too readily to obstruct the purpose the preserving intends, making security of doctrine, as it were an end in itself. Then theologians, it might with truth be said, are doing the wrong thing for the right reason—the reason being the unimpeded accessibility of Christ as Christians love and recognize Him, the wrong thing the defensive preoccupation with the dogma that houses Him. There is a real sense in which we find true loyalty by taking larger risks. Unrisking minds mean cautious trusts and so, in turn, diminished meaning.[31]

The days of militant propaganda in theology should give way to dialogue and a recognition of the religious pluralism of the world.

We have opted for "dialogue," which in some quarters is a bad word. Genuine dialogue is in some minds suspect and met with fear and distrust, particularly because in the past hostility reigned. We do well to bear in mind the possibilities of error, distortion, and confusion that often go with dialogue. However, to our mind, dialogue is the only hopeful way open to us. For, first of all, the incarnation means God does enter into dialogue with man and sets us the example for relating to other people (cf. John 1:14). Second, the gospel offers a true community through forgiveness, reconciliation, new creation, freedom, and love. These require fellowship with others outside the church as well as those inside the Church (II Cor. 5:19; cf. Eph. 1:10). Third, the high priestly prayer of Jesus promises the Holy Spirit, which could lead believers unto all truth, which according to the Fourth Gospel is to be found in living, personal encounter between God and man, as well as man and man, in short in dialogue. Finally, dialogue is the practice of Jesus' exhortation to his followers to be prepared to lose their lives in order to find them.[32]

III

African World View

This volume is meant to be a dialogue between Christianity and African traditional culture. So it is necessary to give a statement of that African culture. That is almost a quixotic task in view of the pluralism and complexity of Africa. In full consciousness of it, I have done a companion volume to this volume. Its title will be *Aspects of African Religion*.[1] That volume, however, does not absolve me from including a brief statement on this volume.

First, let us reiterate that *homo Africanus* is a multiheaded hydra, displaying varieties not only *vis-a-vis* the non-African but also *vis a vis* other species of *homo Africanus*. This is to be expected if Africa is the second largest continent in the world, straddling four hemispheres (both the prime meridian and the equator pass over it). Africa extends between latitude 37° N and 35° S of the equator. On the one continent you have some of the highest temperatures, as in the Sahara, as well as perpetual ice and snow on Mount Kilimanjaro. The resultant ecological factors have shaped diverse physical types of African man on the one continent with different languages and cultures. The number of distinct languages is well above eight hundred; Nigeria alone has about two hundred forty-eight languages. There are at least four major stocks of languages in Africa: Afroasiatic, Niger-Congo (formerly known as West-Sudanic), Sudanic, and Click. There are at least three cultural groups: Caucasoids, Negroids, and Hamites. Truly, *homo Africanus* is a multiheaded hydra and African cultures legion.

Second, in an age when one can fly from Accra to New York in thirteen hours, when radio and wireless are in most homes whether in Africa, Europe, or America, the world has indeed shrunk, and the culture cannot be static. Christianity, Islam, secularism, political change, and the whole drift of the present age have combined to undermine African cultures and traditional religions.

Two conclusions may be drawn from all this: first, since neither culture nor religion are static, we are warned against "fossil culture" and "fossil religion." Second, in view of the diversity we can properly speak only of *an* African religion or *an* African world view, even if there may be similarities here and there—e.g., animism, concepts of ghosts and spirits, polytheism, magic. For this reason we propose in this study to dwell on the Akan world view as an example of African world view, although from time to time we shall refer to other religions.

The word "Akan" calls for some comment. The Akan inhabit the southern half of Ghana, excluding the southeastern corner. They are composed of the Asante; the Bono (also called the Brongs); the Twi groups such as the Akwapim, Akim, and Akwammu; the Fante; the Denkyira; the Wassaw; and others. They are basically agricultural communities, though there is some fishing on the coast. They are, by and large, matrilineal—i.e., for purposes of inheritance, descent is traced through the mother's line. Even here the Akwapim of Larteh and Mampong are patrilineal. They also show a common pattern of political, economic, social, and religious structure.

The first thing that strikes one about Akan society's world view is the fact that *homo Akanus* has a religious ontology. Religion is all-pervasive in Akan society. Thus a good deal of the communal activities of the Akan and other social institutions are inextricably bound up with religion and the spirit-world. Birth, puberty, marriage, death, widowhood, harvest, and installations to traditional offices all partake of a religious nature. Even the office of a chief is a single composite one. He is at once judge, commander-in-chief, legislator, and the executive and administrative head of the

community, as well as the religious head. The chief fills *inter alia* a
sacral role.

> In the ritual as in the constitutional aspect of his life, the chief is the
> focus of the unity of the tribe. His ritual functions are connected with
> ceremonies through which the people express their reverence for the
> ancestors and gods and their dependence on them and also their
> sentiments of solidarity and continuity. . . The chief's position is
> bound up with strong religious sentiments.[2]

It is in his capacity as the link between the living and the dead that the
chief enters the stool house every forty-two days to offer sacrifice to
the ancestors.

At the individual and personal level, the same religious ontology is
met. A traditional Akan would not eat without putting the first
morsel down for the ancestors; nor would he drink unless some of it
had first been poured down to the ancestors. This practice appears to
be neglected sometimes. But it continues particularly when a new
bottle of whiskey or any spirit is opened and at funerals. Christians
have been notorious for attacking the practice of libation. And yet
once when I was visiting a Methodist clergyman who had been
denouncing libation, I observed him before every drink pour some of
it to the ground. After two weeks the clergyman was confronted with
the question, "why do you always pour some of your drink to the
ground before you take a drink?" He quickly came back at me:
"Because a fly was getting into the glass." True houseflies are a
humbug in tropical Africa. But the consistency with which the
pouring of drink was done, always before a drink, morning,
afternoon, evening, and night, make me believe it was a clever
after-the-fact rationalization of a world-taken-for-granted, which is
just beneath the surface, so to speak, and which surfaces when the
chips are down.

Behind all such acts, at both the individual and communal levels,
stands the rationale that a person is surrounded by numerous hosts of
spirit-beings, some good, some evil, which can and do influence the
course of human life for good or for ill. Consequently, their goodwill
is actively and constantly sought, thereby acknowledging the
dependence of the living on the spirit world. In this connection,
Akan society hardly draws any distinction between the sacred and the
secular. This is not the same thing as saying that African religion is

sacralist, i.e., so preoccupied with the sacred as to prejudice the material well-being of the community and to impede man's control over his environment. Rather the sacred, described by Rudolf Otto as *mysterium tremendum et fascinosum* and representing integrity and order beyond man's control and challenging man to the pursuit of development and perfection, on the one hand, and the secular, representing integrity and order such as are within the comprehensive control of man, on the other hand, are not alternatives; rather they are two complementary ways of looking on reality. A good deal of the things which a European or American, for example, would put in the category of the natural, will be ascribed by the Akan to the supernatural. The sphere of the supernatural is much broader in the Akan context than in any European or American context.

It is now time to define further the spirit-world on which *homo Akanus* has this sense of dependence. The first spirit-being is God, the Supreme Being, called *Onyame* or *Onyankopon*. He is *Oboadee*, i.e., Creator, the Sustainer of the universe, the final authority and Overlord of society who has power of life and death. Atheism is foreign to the Akan because, as his proverb puts it, *obi nnkyere abofra Onyame*—since God is self-evident, no one teaches a child to know God. *Homo Akanus* also conceives of this God as a big potentate who may, therefore, not be approached lightly or bothered with the trivial affairs of men. Consequently, God the Supreme Being has delegated authority to the *abosom* (gods) and to the *mpanyinfo* (the ancestors), who, therefore, act *in loco Dei* and *pro Deo*.

Perhaps the most potent aspect of Akan religion is the cult of the ancestors. They, like the Supreme Being, are always held in deep reverence or even worshiped. The ancestors are that part of the clan who have completed their course here on earth and are gone ahead to the other world to be elder brothers of the living at the house of God. Not all the dead are ancestors. To qualify to be an ancestor one must have lived to a ripe old age and in an exemplary manner and done much to enhance the standing and prestige of the family, clan, or tribe. By virtue of being the part of the clan gone ahead to the house of God, they are believed to be powerful in the sense that they maintain the course of life here and now and do influence it for good or for ill. They give children to the living; they give good harvest; they provide the sanctions for the moral life of the nation and accordingly punish, exonerate, or reward the living as the case may be. For example, when a bride is about to be taken to her matrimonial home—or, in modern times, when she is about to leave the home for the church wedding—it is not uncommon for libation to be poured with the following prayer:

> Nananom [i.e., ancestors]
> Your daughter by the name of _____ is today married
> and is being taken to the matrimonial home.
> We ask for blessings on this union.
> We ask for children
> Children in abundance—twins
> Give her material wealth
> So that not only we all shall enjoy the fruits of it,
> but also that there may be children to continue the
> family tradition
> and give you due honor.

Thus the living depend on the ancestors for their children, and the dead are inextricably involved in the Akan family. There is thus a dependence of the living on the ancestors whose authority is nevertheless derived from God. Insofar as there is a dependence, the attitude of the living toward the ancestors is something more than veneration.

The third aspect of the spirit-world is the *abosom*, i.e., lesser deities. Etymologially speaking, *abosom* breaks down as *a*, a prefix which makes a root plural; *bo*, a stone or rock; and *som*, to serve or worship.[3] The *abosom* then literally are the worship of stones or rocks. It appears the word which originally describes an act has been transferred to the object of the act. Whatever the etymology, gods are not always in the form of stone or rock such as Nana Tabir of Cape Coast; they also inhabit rivers, e.g., Tano, the sacred river of the Asante, or a huge tree, e.g., Nana Papratah of Cape Coast. The point to bear in mind is that the gods are not the stone or tree or river itself, but that they may from time to time be contacted at a concrete habitation, though they are not confined therein. The etymological association of the god with a rock may be a hint at the security found in the gods, rock being a symbol of stability and strength, albeit derived from the Supreme Being.

The gods are termed *Nyame mba*—children of the Supreme Being. This highlights their derived nature and their derived power. Their power is at once beneficent and dangerous. Though the gods do not have physical bodies, their personalities, namely their values, attitudes, and thoughts, are likened to those of man. Thus they command the love, attention, and respect of human beings. They also look after the welfare of human beings, giving them good harvest, children, and so forth, and providing moral sanctions for society by rewarding or punishing where and when necessary.

The description of the roles of the gods and ancestors may give the impression that the two are the same. There is yet a difference: whereas the gods may be treated with contempt if they fail to deliver the goods expected of them, the ancestors, like the Supreme Being, are always held in reverence or even worship.

Apart from God, the ancestors, and the gods, nature is believed to have power and even spirits. Thus an Akan may offer an egg or mashed yam to a tree. Behind the offering stands their theory of Reality: behind the visible substance of things lie essences or powers which constitute their true nature. Nature has power which may be revered as well as harnessed to man's benefit.

Some of these essences of visible realities of life are evil forces. The prince of such evil powers is *Sasabonsam*, the master of evil acts. A notoriously bad person is *abonsamnyimpa*, disciple of the evil one. Though *abonsam* is the prime cause of evil, man is not absolved from personal responsibility for the evil committed. *Abonsam's* chief agents are the witches. After decades of denunciation of witchcraft beliefs, it remains a serious concern for large section of Akan societies. The popularity of the independent churches is largely based on the claim of such movements to eradicate and successfully destroy witchcraft. Hence their other name, "Witchcraft Eradication Movement." Witchcraft remains a world-taken-for-granted, lingering in the subconscious and surfaces in crises, e.g., sudden death, motor accidents, childlessness.

The spirit-world which is the ontology of *homo Akanus* consists primarily of the twin pillars of the Supreme Being and the ancestors. In between stand the gods, who can be dispensed with sometimes, and other spirit-beings, e.g., *Sasabonsam*, the prince of evil.

Religion was traditionally the most important sphere of cultural activity that nursed the health of a nation. Religion was the noblest and most powerful force of *homo Akanus*. Today it has lost some of its former place, though it has not necessarily been replaced. Now in Africa, as in the rest of the world, a few voices are heard spouting

Nietzsche's literary phrase "God is dead," and some live in a world without God and, one suspects, with terrifying consequences, e.g., the brutalities that can cripple a nation's soul. According to the 1960 census, 7 percent of the population of Ghana claim to have no religion. Despite the presence of atheism and agnosticism, it still is true that for some 93 percent of the population religion is of some relevance. Thus the population census of 1960 again reveals that 42.8 percent of Ghanaians claim to be Christian, 38.2 percent adherents of African traditional religion, and 12 percent Muslim. These religions have not lived in watertight compartments. For all the changes and modifications, the claim still holds true that *homo Akanus* has a religious ontology. And one believes that the life, death, and resurrection of Akan society will to some extent be determined by the revival of religion.

The second aspect of the Akan world view is the *sensus communis*. Whereas Descartes spoke for Western man when he said *cogito ergo sum*—I think, therefore I exist—Akan man's ontology is *cognatus ergo sum*—I am related by blood, therefore I exist, or I exist because I belong to a family. And a family, which is the basic unit, consists of the living, the dead, and the yet-to-be-born. The family relationships determine the view of man. The unit is the extended family, i.e., grandparents, blood relatives, in-laws, constituting a dynamic unity, or togetherness, with parents and children, according to prevalent mores. It ensures the rearing of children, physical security and comfort, economic cooperation, and social living.

A man is a compound of *mogya* (blood), *sunsum*, also called *ntorɔ* (spirit), and *kra* (the soul or individual personality). The *mogva* he inherits from the mother; it symbolizes his material aspect. The blood makes him a biological being; it gives him status and membership within a lineage, and obligations as a citizen. The *sunsum* and *kra* make a spiritual being. "As a spiritual being a man receives a two-fold gift of the spirit: that which determines his character and individuality he receives through his father [i.e. *sunsum* or the *ntorb*]; but his soul, the undying part of him, he receives from the Supreme Being [i.e. *kra*]."[4] It is important to emphasize that by virtue of the *sunsum* he belongs to his father's kinship group. Thus an Akan belongs by birth to two kinship groups. Truly he exists because he belongs to a kinship group. From birth to death, through puberty and marriage, the kinship group is involved with him and he with them. Traditional Akan society is communalistic.

In modern times the *sensus communis* of traditional society has held its own, despite the assault of Western individualism and increased mobility. People who have lived outside their ancestral home for thirty years are taken back upon death to be laid to rest in their home so as to be gathered with the rest of the clan.[5] Members of the extended family come uninvited and without warning to the home of their relatives immediate or distant. As they often put it, "I need no invitation to come to give my support, moral or financial, when there is death and sorrow in the family. And therefore, I need not wait for an invitation before I call at your house for entertainment or fun." Sojourners in the big towns are organizing themselves according to clans and into tribal groups to bear one another's burdens. Thus in Accra, there is the Fante society, the Kwahu society, and others. So the *sensus communis* continues to hold its ground.

The sense of the community, stemming from the idea that *cognatus ergo sum,* has in modern times been confused with communism. It has even been argued that the *sensus communis* makes Africans more susceptible to communism than to liberalism. I myself am not so persuaded, for a number of reasons. First, communism as a socialist ideology is committed to a hatred and ultimate elimination of religion. Lenin was committed to the elimination of religion. Stalin inaugurated in 1932 the "godless five year plan," which ran till 1936. There is a total prohibition of religion in Albania, "the world's first atheist state." Marxist socialists are hostile to religion because they view it as the bourgeois' instrument of oppression of the proletariat. Thus Marxist socialism and the African world view are basically at variance because the latter has a religious ontology. And one can as yet see no signs of the ultimate disappearance of the religious ontology. Indeed, the effort to eliminate religion in the Marxist socialist states has never really succeeded, as is evidenced by the readiness of believers to submit to torture in Russia, the birth of underground Orthodox churches, and the rebirth of religion in the territories that were occupied by Nazi Germany. That failure to eliminate religion in communist countries convinces us that it will not be able to do so in Africa either. Second,

Marxist socialism is committed to the destruction of hierarchy because it believes that destruction to be essential for the creation of a good society. Even if Marxist socialism and traditional society agree on the equality of men, traditional society seeks to achieve it in the highest sphere of human existence, i.e., in relation to God and the ancestors, the twin pillars of Akan religion. Marxism, on the other hand, seeks the goal of equality of men by destroying all the higher aspects of human life, e.g., communal property, the family. To my mind, traditional society is on to the truth because the existence of individual relationships between people is a fundamental characteristic of human society. Relationships arise in which one person plays an irreplaceable special role in the life of another. And the basic human forces which promote the development of individuality are religion, morality, the feeling of personal participation in history, a sense of responsibility for the fate of mankind. This is what the epistemology of the Akan is about. And it is precisely for these reasons that I venture the prophecy that Marxist socialism will ultimately not be successfully confused with or substituted for the authentic epistemology of *homo Akanus*—that *cognatus ergo sum*.

The two main aspects of the African world view discussed above, namely the basic religious ontology and the *sensus communis* based on the epistemology *cognatus ergo sum*, reflect a third element of the African world view, namely the sense of man's finitude. His finitude is highlighted by his sense of vulnerability to the spirit-beings, particularly the witches and his obsessive fear of death. His finitude is demonstrated by his proneness to evil, which is largely defined as the fracturing of the *sensus communis*. When evil is discovered, the Akan characteristically exclaim *suro nyimpa*—fear man!—or *Onympa ba*—the son of man! The Gă also exclaim *gbomo adasa ni*—the acts of man! It is as if you cannot be human without being frail. And it is precisely because of this sense of frailty and finitude that he always invokes the spirit-world to compensate for his own finitude.

We have isolated the religious ontology, the *sensus communis*, and the sense of man's finitude as three elements of Akan world. These, we believe, the Akan share with most African communities and with authentic biblical faith, much as adherents of the Christian faith who adhere to a doctrine of *tabula rasa* love to deny it. To say Akan society shares these tenets with others does not deny that they are African. It may be another reminder that God the Creator implanted in all his creatures certain ideas and that a number of groups independently hold similar ideas. Such similarities mean we start the dialogue between Christianity and Akan society with an advantage and not from scratch.

IV

The Christian Church and Indigenous Beliefs and Practices

Christianity may be considered either as a faith or as an institution. As an institution it will be aptly described as a church. The faith and the institution do not always coalesce. For over the years the church as an institution has acquired all sorts of things which are neither necessarily Christian nor an essential part of Christianity as a faith. Some of the superstitution and abuses which led to the revolt of Martin Luther against the Roman Catholic Church were not particularly Christian. Today in several African societies, engagement precedes marriage. The engagement ring is not an authentic Christian tradition. Certain attitudes sometimes paraded as Christian may upon examination prove to be falsely so characterized. To put it another way, the mere fact that a stance is adopted by a clergyman or an avowed Christian does not make it authentically Christian. Anything that is authentically Christian has to be supported either in detail or in spirit by the basic sources and tenets of the Christian faith.

Again the very expression "Christian church" is problematic. The church is no uniform institution; for the church is theologically and historically divided between the Eastern Church, otherwise known as the Greek Eastern Orthodox Church, and the Western Church, otherwise known as the Latin Church of the West. This division took

place in A.D. 1054.[1] The Eastern Church itself is divided further into
the Orthodox, the Separated, and the Uniates. Similarly, the Latin
Church of the West has since the sixteenth century been divided into
Roman Catholics and Protestants in their varieties—Anglicans,
Lutherans, Calvinists, Presbyterians, Methodists, and others.
Because of these divisions, they may not have the same attitude to
the same topic. Thus, for example, while the Roman Catholics in
Ghana happily use drums in their worship, the Methodists are
officially opposed to the use of drums. This is a warning against the
danger of oversimplification. Some churches have been more
accommodating than others. And on details denominations may not
agree in their attitude to African belief and practice.

The term "indigenous belief" is equally problematic. We must be
on our guard against the assumed truth of declarations made by
Africans. Anything that is authentically African has to be supported
by proverbs, myths, songs, lyrics, rites, customs, and such, which
are the primary sources of an African ethos. Furthermore, since faith
is never *in vacuo*, and since faith is the faith of a historical
community with all its trappings, that faith is not static, because no
community is static. Through communication, interaction, and
learning, the culture and therefore the religion have not been static.
Thus human sacrifice, which was a feature of primal religions—
e.g., Ashanti religion—is now frowned upon by adherents of primal
religions.

The situation becomes worse confounded by the changing
rationales that are given. Sometimes bogus and fraudulent
rationalizations are given for some of the practices. In 1957 the
Christian Council of Ghana entered into a quarrel with the
administration of the late Mr. Kwame Nkrumah, the then leader of
government business on the issue of libation. The Council
threatened to boycott the ceremony to be held at the Ambassador
Hotel to welcome the Duchess of Kent, who was representing Queen
Elizabeth II of Great Britain at the Independence Celebrations of
Ghana. The reason for the Council's threat was that libation would
be poured. Mr. Nkrumah replied that he would go ahead with it
because it projected the African personality. Of course, this, as we
shall see later, is not the authentic reason for pouring libation.

So as we address ourselves to indigenous beliefs, the questions
come up, How indigenous is indigenous? How traditional is
traditional? This warns against "fossil religion". But it also means

that the subject must be approached in two ways: (a) history—outlining what attitudes were actually adopted—and (b) African-man's religiousness in the flux and turmoil of the modern world.

Two more issues call for comment: first, the relation of belief to practice; and second, the nature of both Christianity and African religion.

Scholars have long drawn a distinction between theory and practice, between belief and worship. Both are important aspects of the faith, be it Christianity or African religion. But in the relatively more sophisticated societies, religion has tended to emphasize belief, the intellectual aspect. Hence the reduction of the Christian faith to a set of philosophical propositions, such as the Nicene Creed, which is couched in the philosophical language of the third and fourth centuries A.D. and which today is not meaningful to many even in the so-called sophisticated societies. The dismal story of the Inquisition in Spain is itself a manifestation of the emphasis on right belief, rather than on the practice of religion. In our own day, many who claim to be believers in the Christian tradition show anything but self-sacrificing and selfless service to their fellow men, which is a keynote of the Christian message.

On the other hand, African traditional religion tends to emphasize the practice.

> Religion, like morality and law, is an essential part of the social machinery; a part of the complex system by which human beings are enabled to live together in an orderly system of social arrangements. That the social function of a religion does not depend on its truth or falsity; that to understand a religion it is on the rites rather than on the beliefs that we should first concentrate our attention.[2]

But even when the practice is stressed, there is a rationale.

We have dwelt on the distinction between the theory and the practice to underline the fact that the jump from belief to practice is a very difficult and tricky one, otherwise clergymen would not be among the worst offenders where the Christian ethic is concerned. The practice and the belief do not always tally. Consequently, as we examine the subject of the Christian churches' relationships with African traditions there may be a lot for which the churches may be ashamed and for which the church should make amends.

Finally, the nature of Christianity and African Religions. We are concerned with more than just the coming together of Christianity and African religion. For both Christianity and African religion, as they are today, are alloys of things. Christianity, as it came to West Africa, is a composite of the teaching of Jesus, Semitic culture, Greco-Roman culture, and European culture. In parts African elements have already crept into the earlier composite. So the issue is not simply Christianity versus indigenous beliefs, but Christianity-cum-European culture on the one hand and indigenous African beliefs on the other. African culture, for its part, has also been influenced by both European culture and Christianity. Thus human sacrifice, which was a veritable part of traditional African religion, symbolizing the supreme sacrifice, is now frowned upon by the adherents of African religion.

The long and short of the story is that the problem is in part to be able to distinguish genuine and nonnegotiable elements of Christianity from European culture, and to distinguish authentic Africanness from phoney Africanness. For example, as of now, there is great uneasiness when a Methodist minister in Ghana decides to attend an annual Methodist Conference Session in native cloth; he is expected to wear a lounge suit. One needs no knowledge of theology or history to agree that a suit is not of the essence of the ministry of the church. It is a European garb. Jesus himself never wore a suit, so far as we know. This is a clear case of European culture being confused with Christianity. Again, when one was a boy, in the 1940s, African Anglicans were not allowed to wear native sandals into church. Shoes were allowed. What the theological significance of, and the difference between, native sandals and shoes is we do not know. Of course, in traditional religion the normal procedure for an officiant at libation was to bare the chest and take off his sandals before addressing a prayer to the Supreme Being. That was a mark of respect and reverence. I am not averse to removing all footwear at worship; what we dispute is why shoes should be allowed and native sandals not allowed. Indeed, the reason the distinction was drawn was that shoes were "made in there," as they describe products of Europe, while the native sandals were "made in here," as the description goes for things produced locally. With this distinction, inferior status was accorded local products such as the native sandals. But this distinction has nothing to do with Christianity.

Let us take another example from Nigeria. In the nineteenth century the Church Missionary Society considered appointing an African, the Rev. Mr. Samuel Ajayi Crowther, Bishop of the Niger

Mission. In pursuit of this plan, the Rev. Mr. Venn, the then secretary of the Church Missionary Society, wrote to the European missionaries in Nigeria to inquire whether they would accept being put under an African bishop. Leaving aside the question of whether it was normal to consult missionaries on such appointments or not, the reaction that came from some of the missionaries was striking. For example, the Rev. Mr. Hinderer wrote the following reply: "The country is heathen and mixed up with and held up by heathen priest-craft, and we are allowed to teach and preach the Gospel not because they are tired of heathenism, but because God gives us influence as Europeans among them. This influence is very desirable and necessary to us; but if they hear that a black man is our master, they will question our respectability."[3] The thesis put forward in this abstract is that the success of the Christian missionary endeavor in Nigeria depended largely on the prestige and influence of the missionaries as Europeans. The corollary of this is that Christianity had to be in a European mold even to the extent of rejecting a black man becoming a bishop, though he was by all other standards qualified. Neither in the Bible nor in the history of the early church do we find an appeal to race with regard to the theology of the bishopric. But, of course, the colonial and imperial ideas of the nineteenth century had now influencd the theology of the bishopric.

On the other hand, there is an interesting statement made by an Akropong chief to the Rev. Mr. Andreas Riis, a missionary of the Basel mission in the Gold Coast in the nineteenth century. The chief said: "When God created the world He made books for the White Man and fetishes for the Black Man. But if you can show us some Black Man who can read the White Man's books, then we will surely follow you."[4] Thus the local chief also saw Christianity as white man's religion.

From the illustrations outlined above, viewed from the standpoint of both the European and the African, Christianity came to Africa in European garb. This is not the first time in the history of Christianity that the Christian faith has taken a cultural mold. Christianity was born in the matrix of Judaism. So its earliest presentation was in Jewish mold. Thus, for example, the Bible presupposes the three-decker universe—earth, heaven above the earth, and Sheol. Today few people will seriously maintain that there is a geographical location in the skies called heaven. Be that as it may, most Christians

today still talk as though there were a heaven up in the skies. That is a
Jewish heritage. To take another example, there is reluctance in
some sectors of the church to allow women any part in the leadership
of the church. This, of course, is in part the Semitic culture's
consignment of women to second-class citizenship which has crept
into the church.

Again, although Christianity was originally born in the Jewish
matrix, it ultimately moved into a Gentile setting. It soon was
scattered all over the Roman Empire, in which Greek was the
universal language, even though the Romans established Latin in
Gaul, Britain, North Africa, and Spain. But with the Greek
language came other things. "The great systems of Plato and
Aristotle had proved a solvent in which the old myths disappeared or
remained only as a conventional vehicle of poetic thought. . . .
Hellenism had meant . . . the absorption of many ideas from the
East."[5] The result was that Christianity began to acquire a Greek
mold. The most lasting testimony of this development is the Nicene
Creed, which is the Greek formulation of the Christian faith in the
fourth century A.D.

And now finally—and to skip centuries of history—Christians left
Europe for Africa. Starting from the fifteenth century the
Portuguese, under the leadership of Prince Henry the Navigator,
made moves into West Africa with a view to, among other things,
preaching the gospel in Africa. That was the beginning of Roman
Catholicism in West Africa. The eighteenth century saw the
beginnings of the Anglican effort from England in Ghana. Later still
came Presbyterians, Methodists, and others. The most serious
evangelistic efforts began in the nineteenth century and continued in
the twentieth century and were mostly from Western Europe. And
so Christianity this time came in European garb.

The long and short of the story is that whenever evangelism takes
place, at least two backgrounds come together. In the case of Ghana,
as in any other black African country, at least three cultures came
together: Christian (which is really Semitic), African, and
European, not to mention the Greco-Roman influences through the
European culture. So the question is, What reaction resulted from
the coming together of the two or three cultures?

I suggest that there are at least three possibilities: (a) *Tabula rasa*,
i.e., the doctrine that there is nothing in the non-Christian culture
on which the Christian missionary can build, and consequently

every aspect of the traditional non-Christian culture must be destroyed before Christianity can be built up. This is the negative approach. (b) The second approach, a positive one used to be known as *accommodation* but now is often called *adaptation, localization,* or *indigenization.*[6] Whichever word we use, this approach acknowledges that there is a whole heritage in the non-Christian culture and consciously attempts to come to terms with that heritage. The second approach is a manifestation of the church's profound bondage to active culture, whether voluntary or not, in response to hostile pressures such as atheism, ideology, of science, material prosperity and comfort, and totalitarianism. It concedes the mystery of the freedom of the spirit and the possibilities for renovation and renewal. (c) Between the positions of *tabula rasa* and *adaptation,* there is a third position, which R. E. S. Tanner aptly calls *working misunderstanding,* i.e., a missionary preaches Christianity in very foreign terms and the natives appear to receive it.[7] That is, they may attend church services, obey church regulations, and so on, without any real understanding of what is going on. Hence there is the juxtaposition of two religions and cultures, the natives interpreting things as they like. The third possibility, *Working Misunderstanding,* is most unsatisfactory and does not lead to any real dialogue. So we shall leave it out of this study and address ourselves to the other two approaches, beginning with the negative approach.

Our starting point is the line taken by the Rev. Mr. Richard Sibbes who has been described as the founding father of Protestant missionary thinking. He was Master of St. Catherine's College, Cambridge and preaching a sermon in Cambridge in the third decade of the seventeenth century. That sermon was entitled "Lydia's Conversion" (Acts 16:14-15). In it he dwelt on the need for preparation before conversion. He said:

> Now, God in preparation for the most part civiliseth people, and then Christianiseth them, as I may say; for the Spirit of God will not be effectual in a rude, wild and barbarous soul; in men that are not men. Therefore, they must be brought to civility; and not only to civility, but there must be a work of the law, to cast them down; and then they are brought to Christianity thereupon.
>
> Therefore they take a good course that labour to break them from their natural rudeness and fierceness. . . . There is no forcing of grace on a soul so far indisposed, that is, not brought to civility. Rude and barbarous souls, therefore, God's manner is to bring them in the

compass of civility, and then seeing what their estate is in the
corruption of nature, to deject them, and then to bring them to
Christianity.[8]

This quotation is most interesting for several reasons. We learn
the following from it. First, civilization, by which the Rev. Mr.
Sibbes meant Western culture, and Christianity, are taken to be
coterminous, if not synonymous. To be a non-Christian is to be in
an eternity of Boeotian darkness. Second, the Holy Spirit cannot
operate in a non-Christian. Third, adopting Western culture is a
necessary stage in the process of conversion to Christianity. Fourth,
non-Christians must be forced into submission to Christianity and
its coterminous Western culture. My only comment on the sermon
is this: Are the sentiments therein expressed based on the biblical
revelation? Or are they echoes of the mental attitudes of the time? It
is true that unbelievers are said to "sit in darkness." But this
metaphorical use of darkness is nothing like the equation of
Christianity with Western culture. Again, what is said about the
Holy Spirit amounts to prescribing limits to the operations of the
Holy Spirit, which is heresy. Indeed, was it not the Holy Spirit which
preceded the missionary to prepare the later convert for conversion?
Further, Christianity is supra-cultural and is not to be confined to
one culture. Finally, compulsion to faith cannot be Christian, for it
denies that man bears the *imago Dei*, the freedom to love or hate
God. Thus on balance we believe that the sentiments expressed in
the sermon are echoes of the mental attitudes of the time and not
based on any authentic Christianity, even if Sibbes meant well.

The attitude reflected in Richard Sibbes did not end with the
seventeenth century. It was even more violently expressed in the
second half of the nineteenth century by the anthropological racists,
well represented by James Hunt, who disputed the claim that there
was a common humanity on the basis of the moral-ethical
argument. He wrote:

1. That there is as good reason for classifying the Negro as a distinct
   species from the European as there is for making the ass a distinct
   species from the zebra; and if, in classification, we take the
   intelligence into consideration, there is a far greater difference
   between the Negro and European than between the gorilla and
   Chimpanzee.
2. That the analogies are far more numerous between the Negro
   and the ape than between the European and the ape.
3. That the Negro is inferior intellectually to the European.

4. That the Negro becomes more humanized when in his natural sub-ordination to the European than under any other circumstances.

5. That the Negro race can only be humanized and civilized by Europeans.

6. That European civilization is not suited to Negro's requirements or character.[9]

We cannot in this short space do justice to the several themes that emerge from the six "testaments" of James Hunt. One thing is clear though—the Negro and his way of life are inferior to everything European. This applied to Christianity gets us to where Richard Sibbes left us.

We refuse to be sidetracked into going into a counterattack on the negative attitude to the black man. With hindsight we see the inadequacies of those who perpetuated such ideas. Today one hardly needs argue that *in vivo* and *in vitro* the Negro is a human being, analogous to the white man in morphology and histology. Indeed, it is no longer really an occasion for wonder to meet a Negro priest, physician, professor, or statesman. In any case, before the white man came to Africa, African man

> knew how to build houses, govern empires, erect cities, cultivate fields, mine for metals, weave cotton, forge steel. . . . Their religion had its own beauty, based on mystical connections with the founder of the city. Their customs were pleasing, built on unity, kindness, respect for age. No coercion, only mutual assistance, the joy of living, a free acceptance of discipline. Order-Earnestness-Poetry-Freedom . . .[10]

In the mission field of the Gold Coast the missionary strategy bears eloquent testimony to the philosophy enunciated by Richard Sibbes. Sometimes missionaries behaved as though without formal education and books, evangelism was impossible. Thus the Rev. Mr. Elias Schrenk, a missionary of the Basel Mission in the Gold Coast, wrote in 1867 the following:

> If we had a nation with formal education, able to read and write, my plans for mission work would be different. But now I am convinced that the opening of schools is our main task. I have a low opinion of Christians who are not able to read their Bible. The smallest school is a missionary and establishes a relationship with the grown-ups, which would not exist without a school.[11]

The school therefore became the handmaid of evangelism. While recognizing that Christianity is a "religion of the book" and while we appreciate the efforts of the earliest missionaries to bring enlightenment to Africans, one would still contest the assumption that without literacy there can be no conversion to Christianity. Formal education is not of the essence of Christianity or of conversion.

In consequence upon the confusion between the essence and accidents of Christianity, the earliest missionaries to West Africa turned their backs on anything African. Thus one of the first things a convert was required to do was to move from his home to a Christian settlement called Salem in the case of the Presbyterians of the Gold Coast, or Topo in the case of the Roman Catholic Church in Yoruba-land in Nigeria. Thus Christians were called out and apart from society, instead of being redeemed in society. Further, this policy of the missions undermined the unity of the traditional society and the authority of the traditional rulers, thereby calling forth their anger and resentment of Christianity as a disintegrating factor in society. It is instructive to consider what the nationals of Ghana called Salem. It was called *oburoni kurow mu*—whiteman's town. The implication of the description is that the settlement and all it stood for, i.e., Christianity, were considered foreign. Basel and Osu (Accra) had nothing in common. Further, as an institution which appeared to undermine traditional society, Christianity was considered a positive evil. Thus the customary rulers of Akim Abuakwa wrote to the governor in 1887 to say: "Now we tell you plainly that we were here before Mohr (the Basel missionary) came, we do not want him or any of the Christians in the Eastern Akim."[12] Or again, when a Methodist missionary, the Rev. Mr. Picot, arrived in Kumasi, the grandnephew of Kwaku Dua I, King of Ashanti, said to him:

> We will accept the Mission, if you act as Mr. Freeman [a celebrated Methodist missionary] did to help the peace of the nation and the prosperity of trade, but you must understand that we will not select children for education, for the Ashanti children have better work to do than to sit down all day idly to learn "Hoy! Hoy! Hoy!" They have to fan their parents and do other work which is better. It is a tradition among us that Ashantis are made to know that they are subjects, altogether under the power of their king. The Bible is not a book for us. God at the beginning gave the Bible to the White people, another book to the Cramos (? Muhammadans), and the fetish to us. . . . We know God already ourselves. . . . We will never embrace your religion, for it would make our people proud. It is your religion which

has ruined the Fanti country, weakened their power and brought down the high man on a level with the low man.[13]

Clearly, Christianity to the Ashanti Chief is a positive evil.

Another example relates to the *dipo* custom, or puberty rites. *Dipo* was obligatory for girls on reaching puberty. It was claimed to be the decree of Klowɛki, the earth goddess of the Krobo of the Eastern region of Ghana. At twelve or at the first signs of maturity, the girl was taken away into a secluded place in the bush to be instructed by a "matron" and priestesses. There they underwent a training course lasting nine to twelve months in preparation for taking their place in the nation as married women. The instruction covered aspects of motherhood, housekeeping, domestic duties, and such. The climax of the custom was a rite of initiation into womanhood. This was the coming-out ceremony, called *Yifom*, literally meaning, washing of the head, at which the girls were dressed up gorgeously and danced to the Klama traditional songs and received ovation. Then and only then was she allowed to go with a man or to marry.[14] It was considered a great stigma to have sex before this rite—stigma on both the girl and the family. Needless to say that as a *rite de passage* it was indissolubly linked with traditional religion, the religion providing the sanctions for the rite.

On the face of it, this rite is commendable as a training in motherhood and mother-craft and also because it checked sexual laxity before the marriageable age. Yet the church opposed the *Dipo* custom. So much steam was generated by the Christian opposition that in 1873 a Christian schoolgirl who refused the rite had to flee from Krobo Odumasi to Abokobi. Again, under the pressure of Christians, Governor Brandford Griffith in 1892 put the *Dipo* custom under a ban. But the Krobos were apparently unimpressed by the ban because the rite continued under a new name, *Bobum*, i.e., clothing festival.[15] But why did the Church oppose the *Dipo* custom?

The missionaries considered it immoral. They alleged that there was licentiousness at the coming-out festival. Feasting there was, but that is far from licentiousness. One suspects that their judgment reflects the humorless disapproval of entertainment and pleasure so characteristic of the Evangelicals and Pietists. And that is not, to my mind, necessarily a Christian stance. Second, missionaries were concerned or possibly angered by the fact that church attendance suffered since several young unmarried ladies were away from the church for nine to twelve months in the bush. Third, they charged that there were idolatrous associations to the rite because it was linked with Klowɛki. Therefore, the real issue is whether a Christian could participate in a rite seemingly indissolubly linked with traditional religion or whether such a rite could survive the breaking of an indissoluble link. But so far as I can judge, the association with Klowɛki was to provide moral and spiritual sanctions for the original intention of the rite, namely training in motherhood and mother-craft and sexual education.

To my mind, therefore, the church did not have to discourage *dipo*. She could have appropriated the intention of the rite, namely training in motherhood and mother-craft and the so-called idolatrous associations made good in a Christian setting, by providing new sanctions for the training in motherhood and mother-craft.

Let us turn to another example: *libation*. In the Akan world view the living are surrounded by hosts of spirit-beings, some good, some evil, who are able to influence the course of man's life for good or ill. Prominent among these spirit-beings are the ancestors, the illustrious members of the family who are dead and gone before. To get their goodwill, offerings are regularly made to them. One such offering is libation, when drink is poured to them. Libation is poured at home, at the stoolhouse, in private, or in public. An authentic Akan, for example, would not drink water or alcohol without first pouring some to the ground in offering to the ancestors. Libation is poured at birth, at puberty, at marriage, at death, and, indeed, at all the crisis points of life. Again, among the Akan groups, the chief every forty-two days observes the Awukudae when he enters the stoolhouse to pour libation to the ancestors. Every tribal festival, such as the Odwira of the Akwapim or the Afahyɛ of the Cape Coasters, has a place for libation. Thus libation is an important and prominent aspect of Akan culture and belief and practice.

However, the Christian church was officially opposed to the pouring of libation on the grounds that it was idolatrous or that there was worship of the ancestors and thereby, according to them, what properly belongs to God. The classic example of the attitude of the church to libation is the dispute between the Christian Council of Ghana and the government of the late Mr. Kwame Nkrumah, the first prime minister and first President of the Republic of Ghana. In

1957 Christian Council of Ghana refused to attend the ceremony to be held at the Ambassador Hotel to welcome the Duchess of Kent, who was representing Her Majesty Queen Elizabeth II of Great Britain at Ghana's Independence celebrations, on the grounds that libation was to be poured. The government of Mr. Nkrumah replied that they would go ahead with it, with or without the Church because libation projected the African personality, Was this deadlock inevitable?

Let us begin with Mr. Nkrumah's stand. In traditional society, the purpose of pouring liberation was not to project the African personality. That answer amounts to saying, "We are doing it and it has no meaning." It is frivolous and superficial and bogus, because in traditional society libation was poured for a purpose, namely to secure the goodwill of the ancestors, not to be African. With that said, let us now proceed to examine the issues at stake.

First, what is libation? Is it just the pouring of the drink or just the accompanying words which express the intention of the rite, or is it both? It cannot be just the pouring of the drink because it speaks something. The truth is, libation has two parts: first, the act of pouring the drink, and second, the words which declare the intention of the pouring of the drink. Obviously the pouring of the drink as a religious rite is by itself neutral. So the crux of the matter is the accompanying words which express the intention. Normally the words ask for blessings from the ancestors. But before they are mentioned, there is invocation of the Supreme Being. The theory is that the Supreme Being is such a great king that he may not be approached directly. Indeed he has delegated authority to the ancestors and gods to deal with the relatively trivial affairs of men. Thus the ancestors, in theory at any rate, operate *in loco Dei* and *pro Deo*. However, one would like to add that as a matter of fact, the average supplicant is oblivious of the Supreme Being and treats the ancestors as ends in themselves. To that extent there is the danger of treating the ancestors as the Ground of Being, the proper description of God—i.e., there is the danger of idolatry. We believe that if the content of the prayers could be made consonant with Christian theology, libation could be incorporated into Christian worship. But as it happened, the Christian church rejected libation outright.

By implication one has accepted the view that libation borders on idolatry. This is in dispute. For quite a few African scholars interpret it as the traditional African counterpart of the Christian "communio sanctorum"—communion of saints.[16] The idea is that the ancestors are not worshiped but are rather venerated as elder brothers of the living. Much as I am most sympathetic to this theory as a method of missionary strategy, I am yet reluctant to accept it as a description of fact, because for all practical purposes the ancestors are treated as ends in themselves, as the real givers of these good things of life.

One last example of the negative attitude to African culture is drumming. In traditional society, drumming featured prominently whether for entertainment or at funerals or during wars. Drums were used to convey messages within a society or to another community, such as announcing the approach of a royal procession or the declaration of war. Since drumming accompanied most, if not all, religious occasions in traditional society,[17] the earliest missionaries assumed that drumming per se had heathen associations, and therefore, was un-Chrstian per se, if not sinful. Accordingly, the standing order No. 548, Section 2, of the Methodist Conference of Ghana (1st edition, 1964) has the following line: "There shall be no drumming at a Member's wake-keeping." And in recent years indeed as recently as 1972, disciplinary action has been taken by individual clergymen against the families of a deceased at whose funeral there had been drumming.

No serious student of the subject of drumming can maintain that drumming per se is heathen or evil. It is gratifying to note that other churches, like Roman Catholics and the Anglicans, have for years used drums at worship.

We have demonstrated that the Christian church in Ghana, and for that matter most of Africa, adopted a negative attitude to African culture and use, being characterized by a domineering and aggressive face. In this way the church created the impression of being an alien institution and Christianity foreign. Hence the piercing judgment of Dr. K. A. Busia, himself a devout and active Methodist and sociologist:

> As one watches the daily lives and activities of the people, and takes account of the rites (i.e. ceremonies) connected with marriage, birth, death, widowhood, harvest or installations to traditional offices, one learns that a great deal of the normal communal activities of the converts lie outside their Christian activities, and that for all their influence, the Christan Churches are still alien institutions, intruding upon, but not integrated with social institutions.[18]

This judgment was made in 1948 and was reiterated in 1971, and to my mind is true as I write.

In my attempts to outline the negative attitude toward African belief and practice, I have indicated a dissatisfaction with that approach. But why did the earliest missionaries take such a stand?

There are a number of factors that come together. There was little knowledge, if any, of African ways. Consequently, outsiders misunderstood many of the African ways. Second, their negative views were sometimes due to straight arrogance, often taking the form that anything non-European could not be good. It was perhaps a manifestation of the Darwinian evolutionary idea. Third, there was also a genuine fear of superstition. This is evidenced by the theory of Probabilism; the probability of superstition was feared and guarded against. So the test is "species superstitionis." Finally, it was also a matter of the theory of revelation. Simply put, the issue is whether it was possible to have a revelation of God outside Jesus Christ or even the Judeo-Christian tradition. They appear to have taken the stand that there could be no knowledge of God outside the Judeo-Christian tradition. These are by no means exhaustive of the reasons for the negative attitude to African beliefs and practices. My own thoughts on these reasons are reserved for a later stage. But suffice it here to say that in the period of the church's supremacy the church apparently overstretched herself, creating cultural values and a new language for religious culture itself. Now she appears to renounce any desire to create new cultural values, and church organization, doctrine, and tradition have become the idol. The church, which should express a living, eternally growing, and eternally developing organism expressing the unity of men with God, can turn into a frozen, mechanical form.

Let us now turn to the positive approach to non-Christian culture, namely the method of *adaptation*. Sadly enough, there is not much evidence of that in the history of the historic churches in West Africa. To be sure, there were isolated prophetic voices in the mission churches of Africa which urged the positive approach. But such voices never had the amplitude to effectively dampen the negative approach to *homo Africanus*. In Nigeria the Rev. Mr. Henry Venn, secretary of the Church Missionary Society from 1842 to 1872, tried to promote the principle of euthanasia of mission, which sought a gradual evolution of the churches of Asia and Africa to become indigenous through raising native pastors and having

financial and administrative autonomy.[19] That never really got off
the ground because few missionaries were convinced about it
enough to carry it through in Nigeria itself. In Ghana the Methodists
have produced and cultivated the use of lyrics.[20] The Catholic
diocese of Wa in northwestern Ghana has succeeded in setting the
sacred mysteries to authentic Dagari music. In the early 1970s
Bishop Peter Dery, then Roman Catholic Bishop of Wa and himself
a Dagarti, conducted a Christian funeral for one of his clergy in a
truly Dagari mode, including dancing and crying. The Anglicans in
Ghana too have used the colorful local *kente* cloth as altar frontals
and vestments. They use the chief's umbrella instead of a canopy in
processions of the Blessed Sacrament on Maundy Thursday. Drums
instead of bells are used on that occasion. The last two efforts were to
underline the kingship of Christ. The Anglicans again have
"succeeded" in translating the English idiom of the *Book of Common
Prayer* into the vernaculars, forcing the vernaculars into English
rhythm and idiom, thereby producing musical nonsense.

Commendable as such isolated efforts are, we are not sure they go
far enough. We are not asking for radicalism just for the sake of being
radical. But the efforts tend to scratch the surface or touch only the
externals like vestments, bells, drums, or organs. It is our contention
that Africanness is something of the heart as well.

Nevertheless, it is something that when the doctrine of the *tabula
rasa* reigned, missionaries on the spot expressed dissatisfaction with
it and sought to commend a positive approach to mission. Two
Anglican bishops of Ghana have articulated the need. As early as
1922, the Rt. Rev. Mowbray Stephen O'Rorke, the second Anglican
bishop of the diocese of Accra, wrote:

> Have our missionary methods hitherto sufficiently been well-thought
> out and carefully planned? Has sufficient respect been given to native
> ideas, not to say Faith and agelong custom? The answer is in the
> negative. . . We have gone to work in the past upon the "unsound"
> foundation that "the heathen in his blindness bows down to wood and
> stone." In harmony with this presupposition, the heathen has been
> called upon to make a complete break with his past and in every
> respect. His "faith" in the unseen world of spirit beings has been
> rudely condemned as "darkness."[21]

Bishop O'Rorke's successor, the Rt. Rev. John Ofeur Aglionby, also
wrote: "It would be strange, if all the nations of the world as they feel

after God and find Him, should travel by exactly the same paths and I trust that in this corner of His Kingdom we shall hold fast to the old customs and bring our jewels to adorn His crown."[22] It may be deduced from these two statements of two churchmen in the Gold Coast that even if, as was said above, the efforts at adaptation of the Christian faith to the African setting were frivolous and on the whole negative, yet some leaders of the church were clear in their own minds of the inadequacy of the doctrine of the *tabula rasa* and wanted to see some adaptations of the Christian faith to African culture.

In the history of missions, two names stand out as examples of adaptation—Matteo Ricci (1552–1610) and Roberto de Nobili (1577–1656), Jesuit missionaries to China and India respectively. At the risk of misrepresenting through oversimplified view of their efforts, let us briefly attempt to draw some lessons from them.

Roberto de Nobili was an Italian. But he spared no efforts to become a native of India, his mission field. He did a thorough study of Brahmin custom and prejudice and accordingly refrained from what would be offensive to the Indians, particularly the Brahmin caste. Thus he refrained from eating meat and wearing leather shoes. He adopted the ochre robes worn by Indian holy men and thus assumed the aspect of a *sannyasi guru*, a religious teacher who had renounced attachment to the world. He mastered Tamil, Telugu, and Sanskrit. He cut himself off from physical contact with the existing Christian church, lest he should become suspect. His mission proceeded by public discussion on religious subjects like the doctrines of creation and the unity of God, recasting his Christian theology into Indian terms, particularly through using appropriate illustrations from the Indian classics. His converts were not required to break with their caste insofar as they were not idolatrous. For in his view the caste system was no more than social distinction. Apparently at first he had some success among higher castes. Later his mission was extended to the lower classes and then began a mass movement.

Earlier Matteo Ricci had pioneered the positive approach in China.[23] It was his aim to proceed with great circumspection and respect for the ancient Chinese civilization. He did a prolonged study of Chinese customs and culture. For the Supreme Being he used the term T'ien Chu, i.e., Lord of heaven. Heaven was expressed by Shang-Ti and T'ien, both words having theistic significance. He also allowed the Chinese rites in honor of Confucius and the family, because to his mind they had only civil significance. And with the permission of Pope Paul V in 1615, the liturgy was translated into Chinese.[24]

This is admittedly a very brief statement of what they did. But more important for us is to delineate the principles that guided them. First, there was the awareness of the need to indigenize. In other words, there was a concern to redeem the Indians and Chinese within their society and not out of it. For the same reason these missionaries did not require them to break with their community. Second, there was to be a sensitivity to the local situation and the prejudices, hopes, and fears of the people. In other words, it was endeavored to speak to the actual condition of converts. Third, the local language was considered an important and necessary tool in communication. This realization was most welcome because "language is the soul of a people." Fourth, they proceeded by dialogue with local customs. Dialogics,[25] which is the essence of education as the practice of freedom, was chosen rather than the "banking" concept of education, which is an instrument of oppression. Fifth, they attempted to concretize their philosophy by adopting some externals of the local situation. Finally, behind all these efforts to indigenize stood a certain humility which did not readily seek refuge in infallibility and was conscious of past errors and inadequacies.

The lesson from the methods of Matteo Ricci and Roberto de Nobili is that any reflection on the incarnation must take seriously the variety of peoples in the church, bearing in mind that there are cultures and civilizations just as venerable and of greater antiquity than those of the West from which missions used to go out. Recognition should be given to a legitimate and necessary pluralism in church life. It may involve learning to value the ethical systems of other religions, such as Ricci did of Confucianism, and the religious values of other cultures, e.g., de Nobili's study of Indian religious values. It calls for openness to what may be found compatible with Christianity as well as seeking positive values in the religions of the peoples to be converted.

The specific application of the principle of adaptation at certain times and in certain conditions was prohibited by the Vatican in 1702, though the ban was lifted in 1939 by Pope Pius XII, who encouraged missionaries to "deeper insights into the historical treasures of these races." Adaptation was prohibited because it was judged to be imprudent, ambiguous, or misleading and inopportune. That method, for all its weaknesses in actual practice, commends itself to us not only for practical reasons but also for theological reasons.

It was again and again the church's practice to appropriate and sanctify the use of societies. Earlier, we asserted how Christianity came to be couched in Platonic and Aristotelian terms, when the church moved from its Jewish matrix into the Gentile world. Besides, even when vessels and vestments were set apart, they were indistinguishable in design and form from those in contemporary daily use and wear.[26] Thus the tunic of pure white linen, known technically as the *alb*, originates in the Roman *tunica talaris*, a day-dress reaching to the feet and with long sleeves. The Roman form was retained, but the *alb* now symbolized freedom from sin. Similarly, the day was sanctified at three-hour intervals in accordance with the Roman division of time. Hence the "Little Hours" of prime, terse, sext, and none.

Second, the militant approach of the doctrine of the *tabula rasa* was not conducive to genuine communication. This was all too clear to some of the Protestant missionaries. For example, Johann Hartwig Brauer wrote the following in his Instruction 6 to missionaries of the Bremen Mission:

> An inconsiderate damning or dismissal of heathenism is no way to win the trust of the heathen and to convince them of the truth of Christianity, but it will rather raise a spirit of stubbornness and obstinacy in holding on to the traditional beliefs, and will shut their hearts to the missionary. Much more useful will it be to find, in the faith and heart of the heathen, points of contact for Christian truth and from there begin the work of conviction.[27]

Now we turn to the theological argument in support of adaptation. The first is the incarnation, which stands at the heart of the New Testament and of the Christian message. In the words of John "the Word became flesh" (1:14). The Logos is identified with the man Jesus. The Johannine phraseology, which juxtaposes the divine Logos and flesh, is most striking. For the flesh signifies man's natural endowment. It denotes the createdness and therefore the weakness of human or animal nature. Yet God does not spurn the earthly, characterized as it is by weakness, but uses it for great marvels and for the fullest revelation of the Word. If the revelation *par excellence* made use of frail, earthly human nature, it may be inferred that it is not beyond God to make use of the natural circumstances of the non-Christian for his own purposes and to his own glory. At the incarnation, the Logos really shared the human lot with all its weaknesses, even if Jesus himself did not sin (Heb. 4:15). "The sinlessness of Jesus . . . does not turn on the absence of human frailty, but in a constantly renewed victory over temptations."[28] God does not shun the natural estate of any man. Indeed, he offers man in his natural estate the challenge and uses that natural estate for his purposes and self-revelation. Thus the whole theology of the incarnation is an argument in favor of *adaptation*.

Another biblical evidence is the whole theology of natural revelation. The New Testament affirms that it is possible to work from nature backward to God. In the Sermon on the Mount, Jesus argued:

> Look at the birds of the air: they neither sow nor reap nor gather into barns, and yet your heavenly Father feeds them. . . . Consider the lilies of the field, how they grow; they neither toil nor spin; yet I tell you, even Solomon in all his glory was not arrayed like one of these. But if God so clothes the grass of the field, which today is alive and tomorrow is thrown into the oven, will he not much more clothe you, O men of little faith? (Matt. 6:26-30 RSV)

Here Jesus expects his addressees to deduce from the situation of birds and flowers and grass the providence of God. Nature itself is a medium of God's self-revelation, in this case his providence.

Similarly, Paul charges the Gentiles with sin precisely because, though they have some knowledge of God, they have confused the Creator with the creature, fastening on the wood or tree as the deity itself rather than as a pointer to the deity. "For all that may be known God by men lies before their [i.e., the Gentiles'] eyes; indeed God himself has disclosed it to them. His invisible attributes, that is to say his everlasting power and deity, have been visible, ever since the world began, to the eye of reason, in the things he has made" (Rom. 1:19-20 NEB). Thus Paul affirms that "the natural man has a knowledge of God, and . . . this knowledge of God (is) the effect of the special purpose of God. . . . God is known because He makes Himself known; He is Himself active in initiating the knowledge which man has of Him."[29] Such knowledge is to Jews as to non-Jew or Gentile, Christian or non-Christian. Creation yields a certain degree of reliable and real knowledge of its Creator to the man who reflects on and contemplates creation. At least the natural man like the one called the "heathen" or "pagan" can sense through creation the power and deity of God.

> Through his life in the world without willing it; he chooses neither the time nor the place of his birth and death; some "power" presides over his existence. . . . Compared with the flux of historic time, this power shows itself to be eternal; it is both anterior and posterior to the unfolding process of history. . . . The power which philosophic contemplation of the world enables us to recognize is of divine character. For it is no blind power; it nourishes thought for the world; it is love; it is God.[30]

Thus the biblical faith itself allows the possibility that the natural man, otherwise described as the "heathen" like our traditional African, has some intimation of God through creation. Surely all the worship of the traditional African is his groping after this divine power, however misguided it may be in parts. Religions, including traditional African religions, would not exist had not God revealed himself, although it is also true that in their attempt to name God, they make for themselves idols, because only God can name himself. All religion is concerned in some way with the manifestation of deity. What is in dispute is the correct method of causing the deity to reveal himself. Primal man experiences deity, at least so he thinks, through "fetishes," trees, animals, or even persons, dreams, and oracles. In some of these areas there is a remarkable similarity with the Old Testament perception of God. For their day they were useful. Now Christianity claims that the fullest revelation which makes all previous ones pale in the background is the revelation in Jesus Christ. As such there is no going back to other approaches now, even if through other faiths, some true knowledge of God has been vouchsafed. This brings us to the idea of special revelation.

Hebrews 1:1-2 reads: "On many occasions [πολυμερωσ] and in manifold ways [πολυτροπωσ] God had [already] in past times spoken to the men of old [τοισ πατρασιν] by the prophets. But at the end of time, in which we now are living, he has spoken to us by one who is the Son." Πατερεσ, literally fathers, means more than the patriarchs of Judaism; it is generally used of men of old, ancestors (cf. Heb. 3:9; Matt. 23:30-32). The word πολυτροπωσ, translated "in manifold ways," refers to the many forms of the revelation of God, the variety of the modes of revelation, e.g., visions, dreams, commands, promises and varieties of content. One supposes some of the revelation of God in traditional religions come under this. The word πολυμερωσ, translated "on many occasions," indicates that there have been many occasions on and through which God spoke to ancient men. This need not be confined to the revelation of God to men under the old covenant; it may extend to the religions other than the Judeo-Christian tradition.

The passage under discussion ties in well with Romans 1:19-20, that God reveals himself in diverse ways and forms. It affirms that there are revelations of the deity other than the revelation in Jesus Christ. But it also insists that only the revelation through the Son is complete and definitive. Thus the divine revelation is progressive, from the less worthy to the more worthy, or from the less mature to the more mature.[31] The text under study primarily concerns the progression from Judaism to Christianity. But in view of what was said in Romans 1:19-20, the idea of progression may be extended back from the so-called pagan religions.

We have been arguing that on the basis of the understanding of revelation in the New Testament itself, speaking of general revelation and the special revelation, we are unable to write off completely the general or natural revelation found in traditional African society, in its diverse forms of philosophy, popular piety, polytheistic ideas, and the divine worship through images and whatever its imperfections. We now wish to return to the subject of natural revelation because the New Testament appears to give some details which may be verified in African religions.

The first principle of natural theology is the doctrine of God. On that broad theme African religions have a belief in a Supreme Being called *Onyankopong* or *Nyame* by the Akan, *Mawu* by the Ewe, *Olodumare* by the Yoruba, to name but a few ethnic groups in West Africa. For our purposes we will go further to outline some detailed affirmations made by the New Testament faith about God.

(a) God is the Creator who has put his imprint on his Creation, an imprint which stares man in the face and can lead to a sense of God. This we also learned in our study of Romans 1:19-20. But Luke as well makes the same point at Acts 14:15-17. There Paul, in reacting to the attempt to worship Barnabas and himself as Jupiter and

Mercury respectively at Lystra, argues that he had precisely come to divert them from their confusion of the creature—i.e., the vain gods which had no real existence—with the Creator and to urge them to return to the living God, "who made heaven and earth and sea and everything in them. In past ages he allowed all nations to go their own way; and yet he has not left you without some clue to his nature" (NEB). God is true to himself in nature.

This aspect of natural revelation is verified in African religions. The Akan, for example, call their Supreme Being *Oboadee*, i.e., Creator. Some scholars interpret his honorific *borebore* as meaning Creator. Proverbs speak of God as Creator. One proverb says that "the God who created disease also created medicine." Or "the God who created life also created death." God is, indeed, Creator in African religions.

(b) God is the ruler and Preserver of the world and his creation. Jesus' references to the care of the birds and lilies, quoted above, make the point that God is the ruler and preserver of his creation. Again in Luke's account of Paul's experience at Lystra, the clue to God's nature is "the kindness he shows: he sends you rain from heaven and crops in their seasons, and gives you food and good cheer in plenty" (NEB). Rain instead of drought which often came on the district, food for man instead of hunger and famine, and joyous gladness, especially at festivals of thanksgiving to God for his gifts to man, are all gifts of God and therefore evidences of the kindness and providence of God (cf. Acts 17:25-26). Surely this is preparatory to the supreme love of God in the death and resurrection of Jesus Christ.

Once more, African religions affirm the kindness and providence of God. In Akan religion, two of the honorifics of the Supreme Being are *Amowia* and *Amosu*. *Amowia* means giver of sunshine; *Amosu* means giver of rainwater. Light, rain, and water are crucial items for agricultural communities like the Akan. Clearly by these honorifics, they express their experience of God as the sustainer of the universe. There is a proverb which makes the point: aboa a onnyi *dua*, *Onyame na opra noho*. Literally it means it is the Supreme Being who protects the tailless creature against troublesome flies. It is the traditional Akan's version of "God cares for tailless animals." This too speaks of the providential care of God.

(c) A third element of the doctrine of God in natural revelation is the omnipresence and immanence of God. In the celebrated speech at the Areopagus, Luke makes Paul say (Acts 17:24, 27, 28 NEB): "[The] Lord of heaven and earth does not live in shrines made by men . . . Indeed he is not far from each one of us, for in him we . . . exist; as some of your own poets have said . . ." (e.g., the Stoic Aratus *c.* 270 B.C.; Cleanthes *c* 250 B.C.)[32] God, through his presence and power may be felt in the world around men, is yet apart from nature, independent of the world and men, and is the source of their life. The Christian's God is not part of the world like nature deified; God is the eternal, initiating Subject and yet intimately present to us.

Once more, Akan religion has at least intimations of it. Thus the Akan proverb runs *obi nnkyerɛ abofra Nyame*, i.e., no one teaches a child to know God. God is self-evident. Another proverb runs: *Se epɛ dɛ eka asɛm kyerɛ Onyame a, ka kyerɛ nframe*, i.e., if you want to send a message to God, tell it to the wind. Clearly God is all around.

The second principle of natural theology is the idea of judgment. In the Areopagus Speech we are told God "has fixed the day on which he will have the world judged" (Acts 17:31 NEB). God created the world for a purpose, i.e., righteousness. So sooner or later man will have to be judged by the standard of righteousness. Furthermore, the natural conscience of man speaks to man of judgment. Thus Paul writes:

> When Gentiles who do not possess the law [i.e., the special revelation of the will of God to the Jews] carry out its precepts by the light of nature, then, although they have no law, they are their own law [i.e., show sufficient knowledge of God's will], for they display the effect of the law inscribed in their hearts. Their conscience is called as witness, and their own thoughts argue the case on either side, against them or even for them, on the day when God judges the secrets of human hearts through Christ Jesus. (Rom. 2:14-15 NEB)

The implication is that non–Judeo-Christian culture cannot be written off in its entirety, because it contains some revelation of God, however, imperfect it might be. Further, since *nullum crimen sine lege*—i.e., without a law there is no reproach—there is the presumption that the Gentiles have had sufficient knowledge of what God wills or forbids, otherwise they could not rightly come under the divine justice. Paul argues that the fact that the Gentiles do at times fulfill the will of God; acting on their own initiative, apart from any special revelation like what the Jews had, is in itself evidence that they have sufficient knowledge of the will of God. Furthermore, the work of the law engraved in their hearts manifests itself by the inner struggles to which it gives rise. . . . This dialogue which man conducts with himself, this debate in which he is in turn the accuser and the defender of himself, shows that, for the appreciation of his conduct, he has at his disposition some objective term of reference, something in fact which God has engraved in his heart and to which his conscience brings a subjective confirmation.[33]

Again, Akan religion generally has the idea of judgment. When something goes wrong, it is often said, *"Onyame botua wo kaw"*—God will requite you according to your desert. Surely this speaks of God as judge. There is another Akan saying *Onyame mmpɛ sipɛ*—God dislikes *sipɛ*. That word *sipɛ* has now gone out of use, and its meaning is most uncertain. But it is suggested it means obduracy of spirit. It and the related proverb *Onyame mmpɛ bɔne*—God dislikes evil—imply that God punishes the evildoer. God provides the moral sanctions.

Our outline of the content of the natural theology given in the New Testament has shown that at least there are intimations of such ideas in Akan religion. There is much in Akan religion that answers to the description "natural revelation." One might even go as far as to say that the Holy Spirit precedes the missionary to wherever the latter goes, to prepare the people's hearts for him. One is reminded of the funeral oration of St. Gregory Nazianzen.

Even before he [i.e., Gregory's father, who was a Christian convert] entered our fold he was one of us. Just as many of our own are not with us because their lives alienate them from the common body of the faithful, in like manner many of those outside are with us, in so far as by their way of life they anticipate the faith and only lack in the name what they possess in attitude. My father was one of these, an alien branch, but inclined towards us by his way of living.[34]

If so, then, Akan religion and culture cannot be written off completely.

We are further strengthened in our position by the fact that Paul and Luke alike used the method of adaptation. For Paul, for example, argued from creation to the true and living God. However, this is far from accepting everything in African or Gentile culture. The numerous gods continued to have no real existence for Paul. Nor did Paul accept without modification even what was genuine natural revelation. For example, although the Greek philosophers

observed the orderly system of the universe, they never attributed the
origin and maintenance of the universe to the one God. But Paul
went further than the Stoic idea—God is apart from nature,
independent of the world and men, and the source of life. Though
Paul alludes to Aratus and Cleanthes, yet he goes beyond "we are his
offspring" to stress God's divine fatherhood, a conception far beyond
pagan philosophy.[35]

We have taken time in the preceding paragraph to outline Paul's
as well as Luke's use and treatment of the ideas and cultures they met
in their wanderings for a simple reason: while we affirm what is good
in African culture, we also wish to warn against accepting everything
African *en masse* and as useful in the process of adaptation. Some
elements may have to be modified or even rejected. It is not our
intention to argue that everything African has something to
contribute to our construction of African theology. For if there is
natural or general revelation, as in our African traditional religion,
there is also special revelation, the revelation in Jesus Christ. In that
progression from natural revelation to special revelation, some
elements of the old revelation may have to be discarded. For
example, traditional society is polygamous. Christanity is monogamous. Here there can be no marrying of the two, although this is not
to say that customary marriage has no validity. In fact we believe
customary marriage is valid as long as the stipulated motions have
been undergone. Only we would insist on a church blessing and an
undertaking to be monogamous. Are we not by this putting old wine
into new wineskins or new wine into old wineskins? (cf. Mark 2:22;
Matt. 9:17; Luke 5:37-38).

By the symbolic language of new wine, Jesus sought to make the
point that not only in words, but also in deeds, the time of salvation
had dawned. The passage is, of course, a *crux interpretationis*. It
should be taken alongside another statement of Jesus: "Think not
that I have come to abolish the law and the prophets; I have come not
to abolish them but to fulfil them. For truly, I say to you, till heaven
and earth pass away, not an iota, not a dot, will pass from the law
until all is accomplished" (Matt. 5:17-18 RSV). Both passages are
concerned with the relationship between Christianity and Judaism
and, strictly speaking, have nothing to do with pagan religion.
However, the principle deduced from them might guide us.

Mark 2:22 does not condemn the revelation of God held out to the
Jews. In this connection it is important to distinguish between the

revelation itself and the system developed from it. He takes issue with the latter at times but not with the former. However, adherence or mechanical attachment to the revelation to the Jews is disallowed because Christ was offering a new and deeper view of things. As applied to pagan religion, the principle holds: we learned above that God had given the Gentiles a revelation of his divinity and power. That is valid and may in parts be permanent. What is wrong is their confusion of the creature with the Creator, namely the system developed from it such as their worship of wood and tree. So the real issue now is to distinguish what is the essence of "pagan religion" and see how far it is consonant with the worship of God as the Christian understands it.

For example, how can the names and honorifics of the Supreme Being in Akan society be used to capture what biblical faith has to say about God?[36] Can it be truly and rightly said that the Akan myth of how the rudeness of the old lady in persistently hitting the firmament with her pestle angered God into moving further away may be used to describe the ideas of sin, immanence of God, and transcendence of God? Even if the traditional ideas are valid starting points, do they exhaust what Christianity has to say? Or do we need to go further than the traditional African ideas?

Again in African society the cohesion of the family, nuclear and extended (the dead, the living, and the unborn), is the basis of the whole society. How far does this help our understanding of the church? Further, the reverence paid to the ancestors is symbolic of the thinking with regard to the cohesion of the family. Whether the reverence of the ancestors is idolatry or has the character of civic or civil and family respect, what aid can it offer in our understanding of the doctrine of man or of death or of ethics? Or what has the whole concept of witchcraft to contribute toward our understanding of the cosmic powers and cosmic Christ of the Captivity Epistles or of the doctrine of sin?

So we are, indeed, taking seriously both Mark 2:22 and Matthew 5:17-18. Put simply, the question is how to couch Christian theology in genuinely African terms and categories without losing an iota of authentic and essential Christianity. At Mark 2:22, Jesus warns against forcing the new spirit into old forms. He stresses the necessity for new forms. Strangely enough, Jesus himself gave no guidelines and, indeed, kept to Jewish forms for the most part. That task he left to the church, and it is the task for African theology today. The form it will take we do not know. But we must be open to the promptings of the Holy Spirit.

In this chapter, we have seen that mistakes have been made in taking a very negative attitude to African culture. All too often, Africans who deal with the subject proceed to attacks on the earliest missionaries. As we affirmed at the end of the first chapter, that serves no purpose, partly because responsibility of a system is always delegated and hierarchized. But one also believes that the earliest missionaries were concerned lest the demon chased away from *homo Africanus* should return with more wicked spirits (Matt. 12:43-45), if "wicked" is the right description of African religion and culture. They were concerned to see Christianity stand out in a society where numerically Christians were in a minority. This concern is laudable. We suggest it is no different from what the Jewish exiles in Babylon did, who, to survive the more advanced and dominant Babylonian culture, adopted an exclusivist attitude. The missionaries were pioneers and in their circumstances could have done no better, even if with hindsight we believe they could have been more flexible and open to the guidance of the Holy Spirit. But our task now is to build on where they left off and remedy their errors. This task that awaits African theology can be undertaken without bitterness. It should be undertaken and achieved through dialogue between Christian faith and African cultures. But it must be a dialogue with a challenge to conversion if it is not to remain sterile talk.

V

Toward Christology in an African Theology

At the heart of the encounter between Christianity and African culture is the subject of Christology,[1] traditionally defined as the doctrine of the person of Christ. The Christian *kerygma* is the proclamation of the good news of how God through Jesus Christ of Nazareth acts to bridge the gulf between God and man, a gulf existing in consequence of man's sin, and the imperatives deriving therefrom. And so, at the heart of the *kerygma* stands Christ. Thus in the evangelistic encounter the questions being posed are: Who is Jesus Christ? What manner of man is he? How does he affect my life? Why should an Akan relate to Jesus of Nazareth, who does not belong to his clan, family, tribe, and nation? These are the matters concerning us in Christology. The answers to these questions determine, to some extent at any rate, the rooting of Christianity in the new setting.

A

In any discussion of Christology, one sooner or later has to make some reference to the Nicene Creed, ratified and expanded by the Council of Constantinople as the plumb line of orthodoxy. That Creed was the attempt of a predominantly Hellenistic society to articulate its belief in Jesus in terms of the language and concepts of its day. A good deal of the language and concepts of the Creed is alien to our current and modern language and thoughtforms, whether in Europe or Africa or America or Asia. Who today, theologian and philosopher included, normally uses terms such as "substance" or "person" or "hypostasis" in their technical Chalcedonian sense? The Creed was, indeed, an attempt to "translate" the biblical faith into contemporary language and thoughtforms. In other words, so far as it concerns us, the issue is to get behind the Creed to the biblical faith.[2] And whatever we evolve should be tested against the plumb line of the biblical faith. And so, what has the biblical tradition to say on Christology?

In our heavy indebtedness to Greco-Roman culture, there is the tendency to discuss Christology in metaphysical terms. The biblical approach is different: metaphysical speculations about the relations within the Godhead are absent. Even the Fourth Gospel, which declared "The Word was God," nowhere speculates how the Word was. Indeed, it soon leaves the heavenlies and comes down to earth with the tremendous affirmation "The Word became flesh and dwelt among us, full of grace and truth; we beheld his glory" (John 1:14 RSV). In the biblical faith, Christology was expressed in very functional terms,[3] expressing impressions of Jesus in terms of his activity. Such an approach seems to us to be on the same wavelength as Akan society, which prefers concreteness of expressions over abstractions. The use of proverbs[4] in serious discussions in Akan society confirms us in the view that functional terms in the discussion of Christology will be the most apt approach to the subject in Akan society. The process of philosophical abstraction from the concrete biblical texts which has been the chief trend of Western theology is not, to my mind, terribly effective in Africa, at least if theology is to engage the church as a whole and not just the initiates. This is said in the context of certain views of the semantic nature of abstractions, concrete language, and mythological/metaphoric language, and the different ways in which they relate to thought and knowledge.

Again, the biblical faith presents us with kinds of Christologies. For a start, there are the two broad formulations of Christology, namely the Judeo-Chrstian and Hellenistic-Christian. Some books of the New Testament emphasize or project the cosmic Christ, as in the Captivity Epistles; others project a priestly conception, as in the epistle to the Hebrews. These do not exhaust the varieties of Christology in the New Testament. This diversity is to be expected because theological formulations, as we learned in an earlier chapter, spring out of a people's experiences and culture. Nevertheless, the diverse Christologies converge and agree on two points: "Jesus is truly man and at the same time truly divine." It is these two ideas that any Christology, whether African or European, American or Chinese, Russian or Australian, Akan or Ga, Ewe or Dagbani, Yoruba or Igbo, is concerned to capture, even if the imageries or terminologies may change. All the christological titles come back to these same two ideas. The humanity and the divinity of Jesus are the two nonnegotiables of any authentic Christology. And so to these we proceed presently.

B

What does it mean to say Jesus was human? First, like any other human being, he was born. Paul wrote to the Galatian church: "When the time had fully come, God sent forth his Son, born of a woman, born under the law, to redeem those who were under the law" (Gal. 4:4-5 RSV). Whatever else Jesus was, he was like other men in that a woman brought him into the world. And precisely because his mother, father, brothers, and sisters were known, the Jews were scandalized by his claims to authority (Mark 6:1-6). He was a Jew, whatever else he was. His lineage was traced through David (Rom. 1:3). In short, he was a personality in history.

However, birth is, perhaps, the least important in establishing the humanity of Jesus. For after all, the lower creation also give birth. Besides, in Semitic as in African societies it was believed possible for divinities to take human form. Left to ourselves, we would skirt the birth, because not only is it inconclusive evidence of the humanity of Jesus but also because we do not wish to be bogged down by the problems raised by the biblical claims that Jesus' birth was miraculous (I refer to the story or theology of the Virgin Birth).[5] Besides there are more and clearer indications of the humanity of Jesus.

Jesus, being a man, had a spirit (נפֶשׁ = ψυχη), without which he was dead. And so it was that "Jesus cried . . . with a loud voice and yielded up his spirit" (Matt. 27:50). And he was dead. By having a spirit, he was a living human being, and without it he was dead. Jesus was also flesh (σαρξ), by virtue of which he was tempted like all human beings. In biblical anthropology it is not that flesh per se is evil, but flesh is the point at which sin finds its ingress. As a man, truly flesh, he was weak and potentially capable of sinning. As Paul puts it, "God has done what the law . . . could not do: sending his own Son in the likeness of sinful flesh and for sin, he condemned sin in the flesh" (Rom. 8:3). Jesus, like other men, was flesh and therefore potentially capable of sinning, sharing with the rest of mankind the consequences of being in the flesh. Jesus was unique in that as a result of his singular devotion to the will of God, to the bitterest end of the death on the cross (Mark 14:36; Phil. 2:7-8), he remained sinless, putting up a successful fight against the downward pulling forces resulting from being in the flesh. Again, as a man he was body (σωμα) in the sense that he had a personality of his own and shared corporeality with other men. It was that personality that continued to make an impression on his disciples after his death. And by virtue of being a body, he lived as a man in a community and society of men.

Still more important in understanding Jesus' humanity is the fact that he was subject to the limitations of all human beings. Thus there was limit to his knowledge: "Of that day or that hour [i.e., the Parousia] no one knows, not even the angels in heaven, nor the Son, but only the Father" (Mark 13:32). Jesus the Son of God lacked omniscience and therefore was genuinely human. Fourth, his finitude was fully demonstrated by his death—his mortality is the loudest witness to his humanity. God does not die! Finally, his finitude was well demonstrated by the fact that whatever power he wielded, he acknowledged as being derived from and dependent on God. Hence his prayers to God before and after cures. His other prayers, e.g., John 14:28 and John 17, also bear witness to his dependence on God. It would be nonsense for God to pray to God!

The humanity of Jesus is one aspect of New Testament Christology which the attempt to construct a Christology in an African theology cannot skirt. The evidences for Jesus' humanity settle down to his anthropological make-up being soul, flesh, and body; his finitude in terms of his knowledge and power; and his deep consciousness of total dependence on God. As outlined above, we believe Akan man can easily absorb the ideas of his humanity. But we shall return to that later.

C

Expounding the divinity of Jesus is a far more difficult task than outlining Jesus' humanity. To begin with, we must repeat with emphasis that the New Testament, unlike the Creed, does not speculate about the metaphysical relationships within the Godhead. As was said earlier, even the Fourth Gospel, which boldly asserts that "the Word was God," at no point speculates how the Word was. The more important issue is what the Word does, for that is, so to speak, a window onto his divinity. Jesus' divinity is sensed or deduced from his operations in the world. And so, the emphasis is on God's relation to man rather than on any metaphysical status. Perhaps more astounding is the claim that "the Word became flesh." After a very exalted start in the heavenlies, the Fourth Gospel comes down with a startling affirmation of the incarnation of the Word. Divinity and humanity are next door to each other. And so, again, the emphasis is on the relation of God to man.

Another striking thing about the New Testament—and here too it differs from the creeds—is the obvious restraint, almost reluctance, in using "God" of Jesus of Nazareth. All such occurrences—John 1:2, 8; 20:28; Romans 9:5; Hebrews 1:8 and II Peter 1:1—are in either hymns or doxologies.[6] In other words, "God" is used of Jesus only in liturgical formulas and rarely, if ever, in narrative and epistolary literature. Thus the divinity of Jesus was primarily expressed not through the term God, but rather through a description of his activities in a manner reminiscent of the activities of God the Father. Nowhere do we find the idea that the Word is Second God in any Hellenistic sense. Despite John 1:1, there is no personal identification of the Word with the Father. Jesus' divinity is described in functional terms. And to these we now proceed.

The divinity of Jesus is to some extent mirrored through his humanity. In Jesus the disciples saw what man is meant to be, i.e., Jesus is the *imago dei*. The determinative theological moment came when the disciples were compelled to say: "What I see in this Man commands my worship. What I see in him changes my concept of God. What I have seen in terms of his Manhood I now recognize as Divinity, my Lord and my God."

To start with, Jesus was sinless. In the Synoptic Gospels, we learn how Jesus was tempted soon after his baptism to use wrong methods for God's purposes and his triumph over these temptations. The

famous kenotic passage of Philippians 2 also mentions how Jesus,
unlike Adam, was obedient to the will of God even to his death on
the cross, a scandal to many. But perhaps the quaint language of
Hebrews 4:15 is unbeatable: Jesus is "one who in every respect has
been tempted as we are, yet without sin." (RSV) This message
affirms both the humanity of Jesus as one potentially capable of
sinning, and his divinity because he did not yield to temptation and
remained sinless. Sinlessness is an aspect of Jesus' divinity. For as
Jesus himself put it, "No one is good but God alone" (Mark 10:18
RSV). And "the sinlessness of Jesus . . . does not turn on the absence
of human frailty but in a constantly renewed victory over
temptations."[7] Clearly the divinity of Jesus is expressed in his
activity, his total devotion to the will of God, thereby keeping intact
and to the fullest the *imago Dei*. This brings us back to the Genesis
stories of the Creation and the Fall. When God created man, man
was "in the image and likeness of God." He was as God. What
marred the *imago Dei* was sin, man's egocentricity and disobedience. Unlike the rest of humanity, Jesus shunned sin and
consequently continued to be as God. He is the authentic man
bearing the *imago Dei*. It was as man that he achieved sinlessness and
thus came to be seen as divine.

However, sinlessness does not exhaust the meaning of the *imago
Dei*. Jesus wielded authority and power, divine power. The authority
he exhibited over nature and sickness was his by virtue of his
perfected humanity. One demonstration of his authority and power
is the cures he performed. Of course, contemporary exorcists and the
Tannaim performed cures which tended to be looked upon as
marvels. Indeed, Jesus acknowledged that the power to cure was
given to other men. Thus when Jesus was charged with performing
cures by Be-elzebul, he retorted: "If I cast out demons by Be-elzebul,
by whom do your sons cast them out?" (Matt. 12:27). There is no
sign of professional jealousy on the part of Jesus. But Jesus would add
that such power could only come from God. Hence his question
about Satan casting out Satan (Matt. 12:25 ff). Even so, Jesus was
clear that his deeds were as vocal as his words were dynamic of his
divine power: "If it is by the finger of God that I cast out demons, then
the kingdom of God has come upon you" (Luke 11:20 RSV; Matt.
12:28). Through the miracles of Jesus, the reign of God was
manifested in the world. And that said something of who Jesus

was—he wielded the power of God. Miracles were a sign of God's power with Jesus to heal and save.

Another aspect of the authority of Jesus is expressed by the description of Jesus as Creator. The classic statement of it is John 1:3: "through him all things came to be; no single thing was created without him" (NEB). Other passages are Romans 11:36, Colossians 1:16, I Corinthians 8:6. True life derives from God through Christ. Jesus is Creator in two senses: first, he is the efficient cause of creation; and second, he is an example and model for the rest of mankind. Creation is an act of revelation, hence the claim that God is knowable through creation (Rom. 1:9-20). On the other hand, as Creator, Jesus is the medium of revelation about God and about the meaning of existence. And by virtue of being the agent of creation, Jesus has claims on all men (John 17:2). That is precisely why Jesus is the judge of the world. His judgment pertains to salvation and condemnation (John 3:17, 19; 12:48).

> During his ministry, Jesus is no apocalyptic judge like the one expected at the end of time; yet his presence does cause men to judge themselves. . . . The judgment that he provokes among men is the one that the Father will accept. It is a judgment that has eternal consequences and will be ratified in that general judgment when the dead come forth from the tomb.[8]

Consequently Jesus has prerogative dignity, exercising the function of God as judge.

The divinity of Jesus is also expressed in terms of his eternity. Eternity describes time that is not measurable or determinable. In describing him as the agent of Creation we have already implied his existence before the world. Jesus Christ was preexistent because he had pre-creational glory in the fellowship of the Father (John 17:5; 1:3, 18; Phil. 2:5-6; Col. 1:15-16). He is before Abraham, the great Patriarch of the Jews (John 8:58), as is asserted when Abraham is said to have had a vision of him—while, at the same time, Abraham is, in a sense, his forerunner. And at the end, he will be there as judge. His life transcends his death.

We therefore discern the following elements in the divinity of Jesus—his sinlessness, his authority and power, not only as the agent of creation but also as judge at the end. And with these go his preexistence and eternity.

D

Having outlined the biblical understanding of Jesus as truly human and truly divine, the task now is to attempt to communicate these basic ideas to Akan society. And we will begin with his humanity.

Sociologists have long pointed out that while Descartes philosophized *Cogito ergo sum*, the Akan society would rather argue *Cognatus ergo sum*—i.e., I belong by blood relationship, therefore I am. In other words, in Akan society a man fully realizes himself as a man by belonging to a society. There is meaning and purpose to his life only because he belongs to a family, a clan, and a tribe. At this point, it behooves us to digress into Akan anthropology.

In Akan society a person is *mogya* (blood), *sunsum* (spirit), and *kra* (soul). *Mogya* is considered a physical thing received from the mother and which dies with the man. By virtue of it, man is a biological or physical being. The same *mogya* gives him lineage ties—it entitles him to membership of his mother's lineage, giving him obligations and rights as a citizen. *Sunsum* is the spirit, which determines one's character and individuality. That is believed to be received from the father and makes one a member of his father's kinship group. It is otherwise known as *ntorɔ*. Finally, one is *kra*, a soul which is received from God and is the vitalizing power of the Creator within one and which returns to God at death. The *kra* also comes to the world with a destiny dealing with the general quality and ultimate end of a person's life. With this brief statement of Akan anthropology, we now return to the subject in hand.

Since belonging to a kinship group is a mark of a man, our attempt at constructing an African Christology would emphasize the kinship of Jesus. His identity as a man was well demonstrated by his relationship to Mary, which gave him status and membership in a lineage and clan. And precisely because that fact was too clear to the people of Nazareth, underscoring his humanity, they found it difficult to believe that there was anything else to him than being a man, living among his kith and kin. And so, the questin was: "Is not this the carpenter, the son of Mary . . . ?" (Mark 6:3 RSV). Again, having a father of sorts in Joseph gave him lineal descent from David (Luke 2:4; cf. Matt. 1:16).[9]

Belonging to a group is further brought out by the references to his brothers and sisters. Jesus had brothers, some of them known by name as James, Joses, Judas, and Simon (Mark 6:3). He had sisters, whose names are not preserved for us by the New Testament (Mark 6:3). It is, perhaps, not without significance that leadership of the early church soon passed into the hands of James the Just, "the brother of our Lord," as happens in Akan societies. The interest in his brothers and sisters underlines the idea that fullness of life consists, among other things, in not being alone. The Akan proverb runs: *Ankonnam ye yaw*—it is a pain and curse to be alone. The fullness of man's humanity is underscored by the relationships he has, a point which is well made by the extended family system of Africa.

Still on belonging to a group is the reference to the circumcision of Jesus on the eighth day (Luke 2:21). This in Judaism marked a child as belonging to the religious people of God (Gen. 17:10-11). In Akan society circumcision is practiced to incorporate a child into a kinship group with its manifold aspects. Thus in the Akan context, the circumcision of Jesus would underline Jesus' belonging to a kinship group and therefore demonstrate his humanity. There will, however, be some difference in content between the biblical and the African traditional views: in our reinterpretation of African theology, the circumcision speaks not only of his belonging to a human kinship group, but also of his belonging to a religious human group which has entered into a covenant relationship with God.

The baptism of Jesus is also interesting for our purposes. Baptism was not only to wash away sins, but also to show his identification with the rest of mankind. Thus the baptism of Jesus, whatever else it was, was a rite of solidarity which went to the making of this man Jesus in the African sense. He was declared a man because by the rite he was declared a member of a group. *Cognatus ergo est.*

The humanity of Jesus will also be meaningfully expressed through Jesus' finitude, particularly his death. In Akan society, death is the lot of every mortal or human being. Akan sayings and proverbs eloquently express this: *Obiara bo wu*—every man will die; *Onyimpa ba, obra tware wu*—for man that is born of a woman, life should end in death. There is another traditional saying: *Atwenetwem di nda; dee bɛba mmba da. Owuo bɛba nso wose odeba bɛba, a, ommba da*—the long awaited arrives late; what is most expected to happen is delayed. Death will come, but often it does not come when eagerly awaited.[10] Death is the ultimate end and part of being human. And so Jesus died and thereby showed his finitude and humanity. In this connection, Matthew 27:50—"Jesus . . . yielded up his spirit"—is very much the sort of language an Akan would use. As we said earlier, under the Akan anthropology the *kra* returns to God at death. Jesus' *kra* was given up to God, and therefore he died, as is expected of a man.

There is another aspect of humanity relating to death. In Akan society, though death is the natural lot of every human being, yet it is dreaded. A saying is that *Owu ye yaw*—it is painful to die. Another example is *Owuo Kwaaku, abo-abusua-dom ntoro a osi nkete hye dom*—"beware, beware, for death is alive; there he is, there he is, he who is a member of *Abusua* (i.e., clan) and belongs to N*toro* (i.e., lineage) and who delights in the wanton destruction of the many."[11] Consequently, there is a fear of death. A similar impression is formed when we consider that in the Passion, Jesus apparently had some fear of death, as becomes clear from his agony in the Garden of Gethsemane. So the death of Jesus in its various facets is a way of referring to the humanity of Jesus in both the biblical faith and Akan Christology.

In Akan society as in the biblical world, a man's finitude was demonstrated by his finitude in knowledge. The Akan is conscious of his finitude because, as he puts it, *obi nnyim adzekyee mu*—a man does not know what the next day has in store for him. Consequently the claims of Jesus to a lack of knowledge about the Parousia would impress the Akan, as it did the biblical writers, that Jesus was finite and therefore a genuine man. This we recognize as a challenge to the (false) doctrines of the omniscience of Jesus which has obscured the humanity of Jesus in traditional belief.

My colleague Joshua Kudadjie has suggested to me that in the Akan view of humanity, one important aspect is the unreliability, wickedness, evil, failure, and such characteristics, of man. He cites in evidence such sayings as *Suro Onipa* (Akan: fear man) or *Gbomo adesa, gbomo adesa ni* (Ga: O man—the deeds of men). These are uttered when someone does something wrong, and they express not only disapproval of the act but also the view that it has happened as one would expect a mortal man to behave. Kudadjie argues that if this is so, Jesus then, to the Akan, lacks an important attribute of manhood, namely wickedness, unreliability. Therefore, Jesus would not be truly man.

We ourselves are not sure that the phrases cited above express more than man's *tendency* toward unreliability and wickedness. If so, then Akan man's version of the biblical claim would be that

Jesus, being flesh, was potentially capable of sinning but did not sin only because he consciously resisted sin.

In Akan society a man shows he is a man by showing a dependence on some power beyond himself. Prayers typically symbolize that dependence because prayers in Akan society are addressed to the determiner of destiny, namely God, even if praying is often done through the mediation of ancestors and/or gods. Thus the occasions of prayer by Jesus would, in Akan society as in the biblical writings, be concrete expressions of his total dependence on God and therefore of his humanity. We would underscore one point: whereas in Akan society mortal man is dependent on God as well as on the ancestors, Jesus was dependent on God alone, showing a uniqueness not found in Akan traditional thinking.

Finally, Jesus' human dependence on God appears supremely in the whole Abba relationship which was so unique of him. Jesus alone was able to call God "Abba," Father, to whose will he was devoted. Unlike him, all other men have become less than human by following sin, which marred the *imago Dei*, as outlined above. But Jesus by his sinlessness is more truly human than the rest of us.

So far we have been attempting to express the elements involved in claiming that Jesus is truly man in Akan thought forms. We have seen that the Akan and biblical ways of expressing humanity are very similar, if not identical.[12] To that extent expressing Jesus' humanity is relatively easy. Now we turn to the divinity of Jesus.

As we saw above, the sinlessness of Jesus is one aspect of his divinity. So we start with that aspect. And precisely there, we have a problem. It has often been alleged that the Akan, like other Africans, traditionally had no idea of sin before the advent of Christianity.[13] The evidence adduced for that view is twofold: first, the apparent unconcern of God with private and perhaps public morality. Second, it is argued that Akan society is apparently a "shame" culture rather than a "guilt" culture because respect for public opinion seems to be the moral force.

However, that impression is demonstrably wrong. For the proverbs of Akan society amply demonstrate God's concern with and dislike of evil and sin.[14] For example, *Onyamɛ mmpe bɔne*—God is opposed to, indeed hates evil/sin. And for the Akan, sin is a factual contradiction of established order, a contradiction which reveals the fault which is often antisocial in character. Furthermore, there is the belief that in the afterlife a personal account is given to both the ancestors and the Supreme Being by the spirit of the deceased. To cut a long story short, we affirm here that the idea of sin is not alien to traditional African society.

In Akan society, the essence of sin is an antisocial act. It is not an abstract transgression of a law; rather it is a factual contradiction of established order. Further, this contradiction or fault sometimes does harm others—e.g., jealousy, murder, rape, incest—and is considered to involve ill will to the other person. The contradiction thus fractures the interpersonal relationships centered on the ego. The Akan picturesquely states this as *eku obi sunsum*—to kill the individual personality of a man. Sin thus becomes an uncleanness, a destruction, and the breaking of a covenant relationship. Consequently, the good life is expressed as *adɔyɛ*—a loving life, to love the other man, which alone produces the harmony, peace and cohesion of society. In discussing the sinlessness of Jesus we propose to do it along two lines.[15] First, Jesus strove and endeavored not to destroy the individual personality of any man—*Jesus hye ne ho do, ma ɔannku obiara ne sunsum*. This, so to speak, looks at sin from the human angle. But second, we propose to express the idea of sinlessness from the divine angle, namely *Jesu ne bra ye adɔyɛ*—Jesus' life was one story of perfect loving of fellow men. One would go on to illustrate this life of love with concrete examples from the life of Jesus which portrayed this life of love. We refer to his concern for those oppressed in any way or form and his efforts to relieve their pain and suffering. That pattern of life in Akan society is what pleases the spirit-world and is the characteristic of the Supreme Being as well as the ancestors, on whose goodwill the well-being of the living depends.

The second item in discussing the divinity of Jesus is the authority and power which Jesus wielded. In Akan society and prayers, the power to perform cures is attributed to the Supreme Being. Consequently a healer, before performing a cure, does two things. First, he looks up to the skies in acknowledgment of his dependence on the Supreme Being for the power to heal. Second, he specifically addresses a prayer to the Supreme Being for his blessings on the venture. Thus the good miracles performed by Jesus would be a concrete way of expressing his power and divinity. *Jesus wɔ Nyame ne tum*—Jesus has the power of God and wields it. He could not have wielded that power unless he had been "ensouled" with God.

The parallel between the Akan healer and Jesus can backfire.

Some confusion may arise out of he fact that both the healer and Jesus look up to heaven acknowledging their power from God. To that extent they show their dependence on God and therefore their humanity. That aspect does not argue the divinity of either the healer or Jesus. However, at this stage our concern is with the end product, the actual healing or act of power which in the thinking of traditional society is impossible unless the Spirit-Being does it. Consequently, before a cure the traditional healer goes through ritual motions so as to be sinless and in a state of holiness, so to speak. At the moment of cure, the healer is not his normal self, but only the vehicle of the Spirit-Being to effect a cure. This is what we mean by being "ensouled" with God. The difference between Jesus and the healers would be the unprecedented scale on which he was ensouled with God: Jesus was in a perpetual state of holiness, perpetually ensouled with God so much so that the divine power was like a continuously flowing electric power in him, unlike the traditional healer, who has the occasional experience of it.

The point about the miracles of Jesus relates to the idea of Creator. In Akan prayers at healings the Supreme Being is regularly addressed as "*Obɔadeɛ*," i.e., Creator. In other words, cures and miracles were evidence that God is Creator. Thus the miracles of Jesus would be evidence that that Jesus shared in the power of God as Creator and that through Jesus' activity we come to know of the love and power of God expressed in his willingness to heal and to save.

However, the idea of Creator should not be limited to the cures in the ministry of Jesus. The Christian message includes the note that that role was exercised by Jesus before the creation of the world—we refer to his preexistence as an agent of creation. That will be the distinctively Christian claim which has no parallel in Akan religion: the claim that the power of Jesus predates the creation of the world. That in itself would mean that Jesus was a peculiar personality who shared divinity with God.

There is another way of approaching the power of Jesus as Creator. Earlier we suggested that Jesus could have wielded the power to cure and perform good miracles, because he had been ensouled with God. There is an Akan expression which might capture something of it: *Jesu ne kra yɛ dur*. Literally it means Jesus has a heavy *kra*, which, as we learned above, is the soul which links him to the Supreme Being. The *kra* is "the mark of the Creator, the vitalizing power of the Creator . . . within him."[16] Thus to say the miracles of Jesus are evidence of a heavy *kra* is to assert that Jesus retained unimpaired and in double dose the authority and power of the Creator.

Of course, there is one apparent problem: in Akan society every man is a child of God. As the Akan saying puts it, *Obiara yɛ·Onyame ba*—all people are God's children; none is the earth's child. That saying emphasizes the vitalizing power of the Creator in everyone. We suggest it is precisely here that the difference between the rest of men and Jesus emerges. Whereas in the case of the rest of mankind that vitalizing power has been impaired by sin, Jesus retained it intact and to the fullest by remaining sinless. Consequently, his ability to perform the great acts of power which other men could not do.

The last aspect we treat under his divinity is his authority and power as judge of the deeds of man. In Akan society the Supreme Being and the ancestors provide the sanctions for the good life and punish evil. And the ancestors hold that authority as ministers of the Supreme Being. Our approach would be to look on Jesus as the Great and Greatest Ancestor—in Akan language *Nana*.[17] With that will go the power and authority to judge the deeds of men, rewarding the good, punishing the evil. Again, in our context we shall seek to emphasize that even if Jesus is *Nana* like the other illustrious ancestors, he is a nonpareil of a judge; he is superior to the other ancestors by virtue of being closest to God and as God. As *Nana* he has authority over not only the world of men but also of all spirit beings, namely the cosmic powers and the ancestors.

E

In this last section we seek to clinch our argument and discussion with an illustration, in true Akan fashion. It seems to us that the court of the royal house in Akan society can serve the cause of Christology in Akan African theology. And we had already stumbled on it when we used the term *Nana* of Jesus, of the ancestors and the Supreme Being. Of the institution of chieftaincy, the sociologist K. A. Busia has written:

> The pervasive influence of religion spread into the political system of the Ashanti. The most important aspect of Ashanti chieftaincy was undoubtedly the religious one. An Ashanti chief filled a sacral role. His stool, the symbol of his office, was a sacred emblem. It represented the community, their solidarity, their permanence, their continuity. The chief was the link between the living and the dead,

and his highest role was when he officiated in the public religious rites which gave expression to the community values. He then acted as the representative of the community whose members are believed to include those who are alive, and those who are either dead or are still unborn. The sacral aspect of the chief's role was a powerful sanction of his authority.[18]

The chief is "at once a judge, a commander-in-chief, a legislator and the executive and administrative head of the community. It was not many offices, but a simple composite office to which various duties and activities, rights and obligations were attached."[19]

In Akan religion the Supreme Being is conceived of as a great, paramount chief who is "so big" that he has to be approached through subchiefs and his official spokesman, called ɔkyeame, who in public matters is as the chief and exercises royal authority, even if it is subordinated to that of the paramount chief.[20] Every chief has an ɔkyeame who serves the chief in several capacities and who, therefore, must be competent in public speaking.

There appears to be some similarity between the Akan religion and the biblical faith with regard to the kingship of God. In the Bible, God is king. As Psalm 10:16 puts it, "The Lord is king for ever and ever" (cf. Ps. 44:4; 47:7). Similarly in the New Testament, God is described as king—Matthew 5:35; I Timothy 1:17; 6:15. On the other hand, Jesus is also described as king, as, for example, the parable of the sheep and goats makes clear (25:32. cf. Rev. 17:14; 19:16). Indeed, his charge had been that he claimed to be king of the Jews (Matt. 27:37; Mark 15:26; Luke 23:38; John 19:19). Thus both Jesus and God are kings. But as the earliest Christians would have said, Jesus shares in the kingship of God and holds his kingship under God (cf. I Cor. 15:24, 25, 28).

In our Akan Christology we propose to think of Jesus as the ɔkyeame,[21] or linguist, who in all public matters was as the Chief, God, and is the first officer of the state, in this case, the world. This captures something of the Johannine portrait of Jesus as the Logos, being at one and the same time divine and yet subordinate to God. Again, Jesus as a chief is human and shares common humanity with the rest of mankind. He is totally dependent on God.[22] Further, just as the Chief exercises a sacral and priestly role as well, so too does Jesus exercise a sacral and priestly function between God and men. Our specifically Christian emphasis would be that Jesus' priesthood is exercised not only on the earth but also in the heavens, just as the

Epistle to the Hebrews argues. And it is by virtue of that priestly role that he brings salvation and forgiveness of sin to men, though in his case he is both priest and victim. It is by virtue of that role that he demands of men obedience to his will, which is the same as the will of God.

Finally, as a chief he is head of a community, namely the church. The chief not only represents the community, but also in him the community coheres. He is the soul of the nation, symbolizing a people's identity, unity, and continuity. And that community owes allegiance to him. For the same reason he is their judge and exercises authority over them and their lives. All these apply to Jesus' chiefship. But there is one new element in the case of Jesus—the community over which Jesus is King cuts across tribal and political boundaries and, indeed, embraces all mankind.

There are a number of honorifics used of the Chief in traditional society which capture aspects of the Christology of the New Testament: *Osuodumgya, Kasaprɛko, Katamanto*, and *Osagyefo*. *Osuodumgya* literally means water that extinguishes fire, fire being the symbol of all pain and disaster. So *Osuodumgya* describes the chief as one who gives a new lease on life by removing all that is inimical to man. The symbol of water is also important in the teaching of Jesus, where it symbolized life (John 4:10). Jesus is *Osuodumgya* because he gives life and delivers from the flames of passion, the flames of sin, and gives hope.

Kasaprɛko literally means he who speaks once and for all and does not foreswear himself. To that extent it is synonymous with *Kantamanto*—one who does not break his oath. Thus the Chief is a determined soul, one whose yes is his yes, his nay, nay. This honorific would also capture an aspect of Jesus, his determined devotion to the will of God, serving God to the bitterest end (cf. what was said above on his dependence on God). But above all, as II Corinthians puts it, "the Son of God . . . was not Yes and No; but in him it is always Yes. For all the promises of God find their Yes in him. That is why we utter the Amen through him, to the glory of God" (II Cor. 1:19-20 RSV).

Osagyefo means one who saves in battle; therefore, a deliverer. The basic idea is comparable to the judge of the Old Testament, who saved his people from the tyranny of their oppressors. This honorific is also applicable to Jesus as the deliverer, but still with a difference. In the case of Jesus, it is not a deliverance through a literal battle;

rather it is figurative. It is deliverance from the inimical forces of legalism, self-sufficiency, and the cosmic forces.[23]

Finally, the Christian tradition has one addition to make to the traditional honorific, i.e., *Asomdwehene* or prince of peace. This title, so far as I have been able to ascertain, was never used in traditional society as an honorific of the Chief, though the Chief's role included ensuring peace and harmony in society. Jesus' kingship consists in leading his people not to military war but to peace, the gift of salvation which Jesus bequeathes to men (John 14:27) and which is part of the covenant between God and man (Ezek. 37:26). It is peace between man and man as well.

It seems to us, therefore, that among the African tribe of the Akan of Ghana a royal priestly Christology aptly speaks to their situation. However, every image is bound to be partial and a half-truth. Consequently we are not excluding other images and illustrations. In the next few lines we seek to show danger in the "Chief" analogy and proffer some modification.

The Chief analogy is dangerous because it is a *theologia gloriae*, lacking a *theologia crucis*. In other words, the Chief analogy denotes authority and power derived from other ways than the way of suffering. In the Christian tradition, Jesus enters into glory through suffering and humility (Luke 24:46 ff). These two aspects are symbolized by the Cross, which proved a stumbling block to the Jews and folly to the Gentiles (I Cor. 1:23).

In the New Testament, or at least in the Johannine tradition, the ascent to God the Father starts with the crucifixion (John 13:1) and reaches its climax at the ascension (John 20:17). The glorification of Jesus was in a sense the reward from God for Jesus' singleminded devotion to the will of God, despite suffering. In short, he entered into glory through his martyrdom. Seen in this way, we come close to a solution of the problem we have posed with regard to the Chief analogy being a *theologia gloriae*. For some become chiefs because of some act of devotion to the society. The big difference here would be that the glorification of Jesus was after his death; while in the case of some Chiefs, their reward was in this life, though through suffering.

The Akan have a proverb, *ɔdomankoma bɔ owuo na owuo kum no*—the Creator created death, but he became a victim of death. I am not sure of the date of this proverb; nor am I sure of the meaning of it. But there is a general sense of deity dying. This may be a myth of the inescapability of death. Whatever it is, Christians may use it of Christ: even Christ, the Son of God, once became a victim of death. The difference between the Akan myth and the case of Christ is that the latter is a fact of history.

In this essay we have attempted to construct a theology of the central issue in any evangelism, namely Christology. In Akan society, as in most other societies in West Africa, the royal-priestly Christology hopefully would speak to most African hearts. But as in the New Testament there are types of Christology, and we insist on seeing the royal-priestly Christology as only one type of Christology. Other Christologies may be developed and expounded. And that task faces African theology today.

The Chief analogy has implications for the theology of the church and her life. An Akan proverb runs thus: If Tsibo (a chief) says he can do something, then he does it with his followers. The kingship of Christ is meaningless unless his followers join to execute his will and purposes. Thus to claim Christ as Chief is to proclaim great responsibilities on the church members, the responsibility of turning away from past waywardness, both individual and social, toward a renewal of all things in and according to *Nana Nyame* through *Nana Jesus*. To say Jesus is *Nana* is to let his standards reign supreme in personal orientation, in the structures of society, in the economic processes, and in political forces. It means in practical terms personal and social justice and re-creation. An African who affirms that Jesus is *Nana* also should relate that message to the issues of human and social justices in African countries as in the rest of the world.

VI

Sin and Evil in an African Theology

It is a tall order to attempt in one chapter to deal with both evil and sin. The two are related, and that is our justification for putting them in one chapter. But for practical reasons we shall concentrate on sin in this chapter, after a few comments on evil.

Christian scholarship has been dominated by the problem of evil—the existence, for example, of natural disasters such as earthquakes, typhoons, and volcanic eruptions which take heavy toll of human lives, in the world which a good God created and of which he said, "Behold, it was very good" (Gen. 1:31). Another example of evil is the inability to see. Evil is such a complex idea and happening that it would be rash to attempt a simple definition. Antagonism, destruction, deformation, disease, accident, death, affliction, suffering, and such—all these come under the title "evil." But broadly speaking, evil is a privation, "the absence of some good which should be present."[1]

In Christian theology the issue of privation appears to be a challenge to the goodness of God and has been debated by every theologian since the advent of the Judaic and Christian faiths. Such a problem does not really exist in traditional African society. For that society, starting with a spiritual ontology (that the world of man is surrounded by hosts of spirit-beings), attributes evil to personal forces of evil, which are able to affect and influence a man's life for good or evil. Thus an earthquake or flood is explained as the anger of some spirit-being at some wrongdoing, hidden or not, in the society. An unsuccessful or difficult delivery is attributed to the violation of family taboo or to infidelity by the expectant mother. In other words, evil is the confluence of anger from the spirit-world and man's waywardness. The two are not contradictory. The situation is no different from Christians praying to God for success in war against Hitler and at the same time saying the gallant soldiers have won the victory. God is the primary cause and the soldiers the secondary cause. So too the primary cause of evil in traditional society is the spirit-beings, notably the witches; and the secondary cause is the man who has done something wrong.

This analysis of traditional society is not without its problems. For example, the suspicion of waywardness on the part of the victim of evil is often not matched by the facts. It is not always that infidelity causes a difficult delivery, and so forth. For all its weaknesses it makes, perhaps, an important point which should not be lost sight of in a discussion of evil: there is at one point or other, human responsibility or input into the occurrence of evil. And that human responsibility is either by action or inaction. Thus the drought of the Sahil, though due to a natural failure of rains, was made worse by man's neglect to take action to check the terrible causes and consequences of the drought, at the first signs of the changing natural patterns. Man failed to pay heed to the signs of the times, by planting the right trees to conserve what could be conserved. Man has been guilty of a "sin" of omission.

Again, the spiritual ontology has its own set of problems. Some aspects of the religious ontology are not still accepted, at least in their entirety. Principally, evil is attributed to witches. But modern African man doubts witchcraft until he is in a crisis. For all the question marks raised against the notion of witchcraft, it appears to be a world-taken-for-granted which surfaces in crises; it is a psychological reality in African societies.[2] Two aspects of that psychological reality are worthy of recall: first, the witchcraft belief is part of the tension between traditional collectivism and an individualism which is by and large foreign to traditional society. Second, the hypnotic power of witchcraft is evidence of man's need to be loved as urgently as he needs food. On both of these items we shall have more to say under sin.

Both points raised above are like the biblical world view: both world views presuppose a metaphysical dimension to evil. That metaphysical dimension is being challenged by modern secularism, even in African societies, but has not been eliminated. With that spiritual ontology one makes no apology for the existence of evil but accepts it as a condition of human existence. Evil remains a mystery to live with. Job spoke for both Christianity and African traditional society:

> I know that thou canst do all things,
>   and that no purpose of thine can be thwarted.
> "Who is this that hides counsel without knowledge?"
> Therefore have I uttered what I did not understand,
>   Things too wonderful for me, which I did not know. . . .
> I had heard of thee by the hearing of the ear,
>   but now my eye sees thee;
> Therefore I despise myself,
>   and repent in dust and ashes." (Job 42:1-3, 5-6 RSV)

William Cowper put the same message across when he wrote:

> Blind unbelief is sure to err,
> And scan his work in vain;
> God is his own interpreter,
> And he will make it plain.

Homo akanus also says *asɛm a Nyame edzi ebua no atseasefo nntum nnsesa no da*—man can never change God's predestined decision on an issue. It is hopeless to attempt to explain evil of the sort involved in natural disasters. We have to live with it and await the manifestation of the omnipotent transcendence of God. And that is why we think it more fruitful to dwell on evil in the sense of sin.

Morality is an indispensable element in the genuine progress, peace, and harmony of any society. Today several governments spend so much time planning for the economic renewal of our states, ignoring the ethical resources of the nations. That course is doomed to failure unless men retain their sense of duty. Dishonest, treacherous, self-seeking, lazy men who are disrespectful of the law cannot work for economic salvation. History shows that religion is the power that most deeply affects a person's life, guiding his actions in society, shaping his conscience. A man is at peace with himself only when he yields to the dictates of his conscience. Thus African

nations, as they assert their rightful places in the community of
nations and men, must take seriously issues of morality, sin, and
goodness.

For yet another reason is morality of moment. There is need to
correct a false impression created by the doctrine of the *tabula rasa*
discussed in chapter 4. As a result of the negative attitude to African
culture by the protagonists of the *tabula rasa*, African society was
depicted as the incarnation of evil. An English theologian of world
reputation and a churchman with long missionary experience
reportedly said on one American university campus in the 1973–74
academic year that he used to sense evil thick and raw around the
temples and shrines in one country in the Third World. That
scholar, if he said so, stands in a long line of mistaken thinking. As
early as 1705, one John Snow, a trader in Cape Coast, the Gold
Coast wrote:

> A black man forgets all obligations but the present; these are his
> friends that *dashec* [i.e., give him presents] oftenest and always. . . .
> Trusting a Negro was sin against the company [i.e., Royal Africa
> Company] hardly to be forgiven. Treat a Negro with a kindness very
> dunstable [i.e., straightforward], there being no people on earth that
> you can gain a point sooner of than the black, if soft and easy methods
> are used. All other methods of violence serve only to raise devils that
> none as yet has had the good fortune to lay.[3]

The message is that the blacks are *inter alia* morally bankrupt, not
trustworthy, and by nature men of violence. Also in the eighteenth
century the first Anglican missionary to the Gold Coast, the Rev.
Mr. Thomas Thompson said of the Fante of the Gold Coast, "As to
their sense of vices and virtues they have only cold and unaffecting
notions of both. . . . Spiritual matters made no impressions on
them."[4] We shall see later that this is not true to the facts of the
history and cultures of Africa. But both Snow and Thompson, like
the contemporary theologian mentioned above, are representatives
of a long line of Western students of Africa who have claimed that
before the advent of Christianity, Africans had no sense of sin[5] or at
the best belonged to a shame culture.[6] To them, sin is Negro as
virtue is White.

Scholars have suggested that primal societies such as the
traditional African societies have a "shame culture" in contradis-
tinction to "guilt culture" (e.g., Judaism and Christianity) because

the *summum bonum* of the former is the enjoyment of time and public esteem and not a quiet conscience. In other words, the strongest moral force in a shame-culture is respect for public opinion rather than the fear of God. It is further alleged that transition is made from a shame culture to a culture of guilt only under the impact of a growing political and economic insecurity, which in turn deepens the awareness of human helplessness and religious anxiety.

I myself am not impressed with these arguments. For one thing, it is just not true that guilt is related to growing political and economic insecurity. It is so-called political giants who exploited relatively simple Africans, without any sense of shame or guilt. And it was members of the same group that in this century murdered six million Jews for no good reason. Furthermore, if the Creator God did not leave the world without his stamp, as is asserted by the theology of natural revelation, then it is impossible that the non-Christians who practiced African traditional religion should be without a sense of good and evil. The worst that could be said would relate to the clarity and depth of that sense of good and evil. Besides, there is more positive evidence that traditional African societies had moral sense.

First, it is not true that the *summum bonum* of African society is the enjoyment of time and public esteem rather than a quiet conscience. That false notion is contradicted by the Akan *Tiboa*[7] (Fante *Tsiboaba*), i.e., conscience. Literally, *tiboa* means animal in the head, a being existing by itself which originates any strong commotion in the head. It is the inward voice, or conscience. A Fante proverb runs *wo tsiboaba bɔ wo kɔkɔ na anntse a, ɔtsea wo*—if you do not heed the warning of your conscience, it punishes you. An Asante version of it is *worekɔyɛ bɔne bi a, wo tiboa ka kyerɛ wo se: ŋkɔyɛ! na sɛ wubu so kɔyɛ a, na wo tiboa haw wo*—if a man is about to commit some evil, his conscience says to him "do not do it." But if he ignores that warning and persists in committing the evil, his conscience torments him. On the basis of these two variant proverbs it can be asserted that in Akan society also the *summum bonum* is a quiet conscience. There is no basis for classifying Akan culture as a shame culture.[8]

Second, other proverbs and sayings indicate that in Akan society *Onyankopɔn*, the Supreme Being, though apparently a *deus coelestis*,[9] is concerned with both public and private morality. The Akan say *Onyame mmpɛ bɔne*—God hates evil. Or again, an aggrieved person often says to his offender, *Onyame botua wo kaw*—God will punish you for your wicked deed. The conclusion to be drawn from such sayings is that in the Akan world view God is concerned with and about evil and acts in judgment sooner or later to put right the balance. What happens between two men apparently involves God.

A third important evidence is that concept of *nkrabea*, literally the manner (*bea*) of the *kra* (ego). According to the Akan world view, a man's *kra*, or ego, takes leave of God to be a man on earth with a *krabea*, destiny or the predestined plan of the general quality and ultimate end of his life. For a start, the *nkrabea* is the ego ideal, the image of the self, which implies a continual moral imperative. Furthermore, this *kra*, or life-soul, which is received from God, returns to God to render account of himself to his King, God. [10]

Fourth, Akan man's belief in the ancestors includes the idea that the ancestors provide the sanctions for the good life at least within the clan and tribe. Thus if a well-to-do member of the clan fails to minister to the needs of the less fortunate in the family, it is believed the ancestors would punish him. The clan exhorts men to *adɔyɛ*—loving one another—as demanded by the ancestors who are the second pillar of Akan religion.

In view of the four facts laid out above, one can only conclude that the claim that African societies such as the Akan had no sense of sin before the advent of Christianity is misguided and unfounded. So for our purposes the real issue is whether in detail Akan ethics and Christian ethics can travel together or be complementary, and which aspects are unacceptable to genuine Christian conscience.

The proclamation of the gospel, among other things, convicts people of sin and brings about a sense of wrongness. The earliest kerygma always contained the call to "repent and be baptized in the name of Christ." Down the centuries, there have been some striking aberrations to the call to repent. For example, in some popular versions of Christianity, especially under the impact of pietism and the evangelical revival, there is a tendency to treat sin only in its vertical aspect, i.e., in terms of God and his laws and often underplaying the horizontal dimension of religion and sin, i.e., the reflection of the God-ward dimension in the world of men. Consequently, sin for these versions of Christianity tends to be essentially of a private character, e.g., fornication, drunkenness, dancing, gambling, swearing. These, to my mind, are only a limited range of moral offences and divert attention from those areas where ethical inspection would create tensions for the smooth operation of the system. In any authentic biblically based African theology the vertical and horizontal dimensions of religion and sin have to be held in balance. For the biblical faith leaves us in no doubt that he is a liar who professes to love God but hates his fellowman. If he is unable to love his fellowman whom he sees everyday, he cannot truly love God, whom he never sees. To treat religion and morality as a private matter alone is to violate authentic biblical faith.

One manifestation of this false teaching is the tendency to separate religion and morality from the rest of life. It is not uncommon to hear such statements as: "Keep religion out of politics" or "Economic man has no place for religion." Those who promote such distinctions are trying in effect to get rid of religion altogether, for they do not wish religion to interfere with the way they live. A society which treats religion as unrelated to the conduct of public life is soon swallowed up in corruption, violence, and sin. The atrocities of Auschwitz, Dachau in Nazi Germany, and the cruel brutalities and corruption of Mr. Nkrumah's Ghana certainly illustrate that lesson.[11] There can be no valid neutrality for the Christian in public life.

A second confusion is the confusion between the demands of the church and the demands of conscience, e.g., the use of the pill in birth control, and the consumption of alcoholic beverages. The situation has been worse confounded by the impact of the evangelical revival, which in the nineteenth century was character-ized by a rather ostentatious piety, a strong social conscience, extreme respectability, and a somewhat humorless disapproval of entertainment and pleasure. Respectability should not be confused with righteousness. The demands of the church may lead to respectability without necessarily leading to goodness. The Pharisee, after his vote of self-confidence for having successfully followed the minutiae of the Jewish church-state, was still found wanton and wanting in the scales of God.

Again, some people talk as if morality is the preserve of Christians and write off all non-Christians as immoral. This to my mind is false. For the sense of right and wrong can never be completely rooted out of normal human nature, which God himself has created. However depraved a man may be, he is still attracted instinctively to goodness.

Down the centuries, Christians have been noted for habitually condemning society for sin. Some would suggest that much of modern music, which in their ears is distinguished by barbaric primitivity and loathsome cacophony, is evidence of the sin of the world. Traditionally, Christian preachers have presented the world as hell-bent on self-destruction. They see evidence *inter alia* in the current fear of thermonuclear holocaust. An aspect of their viewpoint is the tendency to treat God as the "God of the gaps," dragged in only when we do not have the technique for handling situations. It is gratifying to note that from within the church voices of protest have been raised against the tendency to treat the world outside the Christian church as hell-bent on destruction. The best representative of these voices of protest is the late Dietrich Bonhoeffer, who tasted Nazi wickedness to the dregs, dying a martyr's death only months before the defeat of the Nazis in 1945.

In his *Letters and Papers from Prison*, Bonhoeffer protested against the all too negative attitude of Christians toward the world outside the church and pleaded that the world be approached from its strong points rather than its weaknesses. To him the process toward the autonomy of man, begun in about the thirteenth century, has come to completion in the twentieth century. By the autonomy of man he means the discovery of the laws by which the world lives and manages in science, social and political affairs, art, ethics, and religion. Man has been coping with most of his problems in these areas without recourse to the God hypothesis. He therefore exhorts Christians to recognize that "the world has come of age," i.e., men should now live on the basis of what they have come to know over the past seven centuries at least, and not on the basis of irrational religious taboos; men are called to freedom and responsibility. As he puts it:

> One must abandon every attempt to make something of oneself, whether it be a saint, a converted sinner, a churchman [the priestly type, so-called!], a righteous man or an unrighteous one, a sick man or a healthy one. This is what I mean by worldliness—taking life in one's stride, with all its duties and problems, its successes and failures, its experiences and helplessness. It is in such a life that we throw ourselves utterly into the arms of God, and participate in his sufferings in the world and watch with Christ in Gethsemane.[12]

To this protest, for all its difficulties, we add our voice. we add still further that some of the hell-fire theology often heard from the pulpits is a form of manipulation of man, which is bad, whether it comes from religious circles or atheistic politicians and economists.

Alongside that protest with which we have concurred, we, again with Bonhoeffer, also affirm the reality of evil and sin in the world. And Bonhoeffer drank the cup of Nazi sinfulness and evil to the bitterest end. We are convinced that the New Testament, and through it the Christian tradition, has a true and penetrating and perceptive diagnosis of the condition of man as a sinner. "All men have sinned" (Rom. 3:23, cf. I John 1:8). This is so at both individual and corporate levels. For example, the League of Nations and its successor body, the United Nations, have been talking of peace for decades, and yet we seem none the nearer to peace, despite all sorts of documents signed by the nations of the world. In Africa there has been uneasiness between member states of the Organisation of the African Unity resulting in much carnage and wastage of badly needed resources, both human and material: Ethiopia versus Somalia, Uganda versus Tanzania, Uganda versus Kenya, Ghana versus Guinea, Ghana versus Togoland, and so on. Nigeria saw much carnage and wanton destruction of her resources as a result of a cruel and bloody civil war lasting from 1967 to 1970. Bribery and corruption are front-page news in Africa as in America, in Asia as in Europe, resulting in military coups d'état in African countries and Latin American countries, in the resignation of government officials, and of the overthrow of governments elsewhere in the world. The Lockheed corruption scandal in 1976 led to the stripping of a prince in Holland and the prosecution of a former prime minister of Japan. The Shylocks and Macbeths are still portrayed in the world every day and in every society. Common to all these is selfishness of individuals as well as of states. So no apology is made for accepting the penetrating and perceptive biblical analysis of the condition of man as a sinner. What then do we understand by sin?

Sin is a big and complex theme in the Bible, as is evidenced by the diverse terms used for it. Presumably each of these terms highlights a particular aspect of sin. Together they reveal the many-sidedness of sin. We shall go through some of the key ones.

First, sin is conceived as a *debt* (Greek, *opheilema* = Hebrew, *Choba*). That metaphor highlights sin as the failure to pay back to God the reverence due to him and which is expressed through obedience and glad submission to the divine will. That reverence is owed to God because we believe God to be the ground of our being:

"in him we move, live and have our being" (Acts 17:24-28). That failure to acknowledge by word and deed that God is the ground of being is sin (Matt. 6:12; 18:23-35; Mic. 6:6-8). Since man owes everything to God, he has a duty, an obligation toward God, to obey the divine will. To deviate from the way God has prescribed for man is to sin, to owe him a debt. This creditor-debtor relationship between God and man may be confined or disrupted by the performance or nonperformance of God's will. The disruption is what is termed sin. However, it is also important to add that in the New Testament "the idea of debts develops out of a more profound view (than the legal idea of debt), namely that the relationship between God and man is a personal one, not bound by a rigid necessity."[13]

This metaphor has its counterpart in Akan society. Earlier we quoted the Akan saying *Nyame botua wo kaw*, a statement often made by an offended party to or about the offender. *Tua kaw* means to fill up or replace what is wanting: to pay a debt, to make amends, to pay damages, and to punish. To wrong a neighbor is to incur a debt which God fills up by the punishment he metes out to the offender. Further, the basic conception of God as King in traditional Akan society implies the idea of obligations on the part of men, God's subjects. Thus the debt metaphor for sin in the biblical faith is already meaningful to the Akan. It is proposed, therefore, one of the metaphors to be used of sin in an African theology is that of debt. When a man sins, *ɔdze Onyame kaw*—he owes God a debt, which has to be paid up somehow.

The second term is backsliding (Greek *Planē*)(e.g., Heb. 3:10, 15; I John 1:8; 4:6). This metaphor projects sin as a straying from a norm. It is an error or deceit. Akan society also has the same metaphor for a type of evil. For the same idea, Akan man has *nnabraba* (Twi, cf. Fante, *ndabraba*)—deceit.[14] It highlights sin as hypocrisy, a lie, the life of an imposter. Following the same metaphor Satan will be *ɔdabrabafo*.

A third word is trespass (Greek, *paraptōma* = Hebrew *Ma'al* or *pesha'* or *'awel*—e.g., Rom. 5:15; Mark 11:25; Matt. 6:14.) Etymologically speaking, to trespass *(parapiptein)* is to fall beside or aside, presumably an approved path; it is to stumble. The Greek root word gives the impression of sin as an accidental error, albeit a culpable mistake (cf. Ezek. 18:24; 14:13; 15:8). In this connection Romans 5:20 is interesting: "Law intruded into this process to multiply law-breaking" (NEB; Greek *paraptōma*). The idea is that sin was in the world before the Jewish Torah was given. Thereafter, lack of knowledge of the law cannot excuse sin. The law only reveals sin and sinfulness more vividly than otherwise. Be that as it may, *paraptōma* refers to "the disruption of man's relation to God through his fault."[15]

Next door to trespass is *ignorance* (Greek, *agnoēma*). This occurs only at Hebrews 9:7. It may be translated sin of inadvertence, though it is still culpable—cf. Luke 23:34; I Tim. 1:13.

A fifth major term is *transgression* (Greek, *Parabasis*). It occurs seven times in the entire New Testament (Rom. 2:23; 4:15; 5:14; Gal. 3:19; I Tim. 2:14; Heb. 2:2; 9:15). It is predominantly a Pauline word. The cognate verb *parabainein* occurs three times in the New Testament in the sense of to transgress (Matt. 15:2, 3; Acts 1:25). That root literally means to stride to and fro, presumably in a line. The line in this context is the law. Thus transgression speaks of sin in its relation to the law: "Where there is no law there can be no breach of law" (*parabasis*) (Rom. 4:15 NEB). The law is a correlative of *parabasis* or transgression. "The possession of the law is not the cause of transgression but it brings to light the essential character of the latter."[16] The law "was added to make wrongdoing a legal offence" (Gal. 3:19 NEB).[17]

Traditional Akan society's expression for transgress is *fom mmarasa so* and its synonym *tōmmara*—to transgress or trespass on the law. Akan society also asserts that knowledge of the law is a correlative of transgression. For his maxim is *ɔhɔho nto mmara*, literally, the stranger does not break the law. It does not mean that he is not culpable; rather the stranger may not be penalized when he breaks the law, because he is ignorant or not conscious of the laws and conventions of the land.

Insofar as transgression is a direct violation of a divine law, it relates to a number of other words—*hettēma*, *parakoē*, and *anomia*, all of which are Greek words. *Hettēma* occurs only twice in the New Testament, at Romans 11:12 and I Corinthians 6:7. It means diminishing what should have been rendered in full measure, presumably to God. For our purposes, I Corinthians 6:7 is the significant passage because it is used in an ethical sense: "you already fall below your standard in going to law with one another at all" (NEB). "The very existence of disputes between Christians is in itself already a moral defeat."[18]

Parakoē, translated disobedience, occurs three times (Rom. 5:19; II Cor. 10:6; Heb. 2:2). The word emphasizes two aspects of sin: (a) a "positive aspect of trespassing on a forbidden ground" and (b) a "negative aspect of disobeying a lawful command."[19] But the emphasis is on the negative aspect. Insofar as *parakoē* underlines the disobedience of an express command of God and thus underlines the heinousness of sin, Adam becomes the paradigm of disobedience and the antitype of Jesus Christ, who "was obedient unto death, even death on a cross" (Phil. 2:8 RSV).

Anomia means lawlessness—Matthew 7:23; 13:41; 23:28; 24:12; Romans 4:7; 6:19; II Corinthians 6:14; II Thessalonians 2:3, 7; Hebrews 1:9; 10:17; Titus 2:14; I John 3:4. By this word, sin is depicted as the violation of the divine law. "It is the assertion of the selfish will against a paramount authority," namely the law, "which expresses the divine ideal of man's constitution and growth."[20] Human will is disobedient and hostile in act, word, and intention to the imperative divine will.

By far the commonest word for sin is *hamartia* (Hebrew, *chatt'ath*, *'on*, *pesha'*, and *'asham*).[21] *Hamartia* is the principle of which sinful acts are several manifestations. It is a metaphor from shooting. *Hamartia* is missing the mark, whether mistakenly or guiltily. It covers anything from crimes to harmless faults. It is used both of *peccatio* (Latin), i.e., the act of sinning, and of *peccatum*, i.e., the sin actually committed.

This survey of the words for sin does not exhaust the list in the New Testament. There are others we have not touched: e.g., malice (Greek, *kakia*; Rom. 1:29; Tit. 3:3); active mischief (Greek, *ponēria*; Mark 7:22; Rom. 1:29, I Cor. 5:8); wickedness (Greek, *adikia*; Rom. 6:13). But the survey would at least suggest that sin is a big theme, which the biblical faith puts across in diverse metaphors. It may be thought of legalistically (e.g., a debt, transgression, lawlessness) or in a homely way, as at Luke 15:18-21, namely that sin is a going out of the Father's house and remoteness from God. Whichever metaphor it is, sin is a falling short of a mark, namely the glory of God or the image and likeness of God (cf. Rom. 3:23). Sin is the deprivation of the presence of God and of communion with God.

Akan ethics does not have this rich diversity of terms for sin and goodness. Nor do we believe it should follow the biblical example to create a store of vocabulary for expressing ethical concepts. What there is, we believe to be adequate. Virtue or goodness is described with three Akan words—*pa, papa, yie. Pa,* meaning good, "is always compounded . . . with a noun to which it is conjoined, so that the noun has a low tone throughout"[22]—e.g., *onipa-pa,* a good man; *koma-pa,* a good heart. It has the force of what is proper, true, real, genuine. Its reduplicated form is *papa*—good things, moral good, good action, goodness, kindness, well-being, as well as good luck.[23] Goodness, then, is not an abstract concept but an action or activity or act which displays the well-being of the doer and shows kindness to another.[24] But when virtue is considered as a qualitative good, abstract and spiritual, it is the quality of God, the source of *depa*—good actions. The Akan say *papa yɛ Nyamesu a edi kan*—goodness is the foremost nature of God. But virtue is sustained in things, actions, and circumstances, and manifests itself in such attributes as *trenee* (also spelled *terenee*)—straight or just; *krɔnkrɔn*—pure, unadulterated; *babunnye*—pure, virgin, and healthy; *hotewee*—clean, bright. Thus virtue has to do with holiness, sanctity, purity, and cleanliness. What is good is beautiful. Virtue is not only an individual affair; it also has social implications since Akan man's theory of existence is *cognatus ergo sum*—I am related by blood, therefore I exist. Thus virtue maintains the communalistic society rather than the individual.

Vice is *bɔne*—wickedness—an unkind act or word or thought. Akan society tends to see *bɔne* not in abstract terms but as acts. And since his theory of existence is *cognatus ergo sum, bɔne* is often against another person in the society or the society as a whole. The Akan says *mayɛ bɔne*—I have done evil, or I have sinned. Sin is any act, motivation, or conduct which is directed against the *sensus communis,* the social harmony and the personal achievement sanctioned by the traditional code.

Though the sins are against an individual or the society in the first instance, Akan society believes them also to be against the ancestors and God. For these provide the sanctions for the good life. It is precisely because of this that it is often said *Onyame botua wo kaw*—God will punish you according to your deeds/deserts. And it is also precisely for this reason that it is believed that the one who neglects to discharge his responsibilities to the less fortunate of the family is punished by the ancestors with some calamity, e.g., death, *saman-yarba* (disease caused by the ghost), and so forth. And therefore, in Akan society sin is against the spirit-world as well.

Akan society relates sin to the personality. It proceeds out of a man's heart: *ɔdwen ne komâm bɔne*—he thinks evil in his heart or devises (contrives) evil in his heart, which in Akan society is the center of the bodily system as well as of the affections. Sin, therefore, is one manifestation of one's being: thus when a man is given to anger, they say *ɔyare koma*, literally, he has a sick heart. Sometimes language is used which may suggest the personification of evil: *ne bɔne a ekura no*—his sin has possessed him. It is as if he cannot resist sinning. To this we shall return when we turn to Satan.

Other metaphors are used of sin. We have mentioned the idea of sin as a debt to God as well as a violation, witting or unwitting, of God's or society's norms. In this connection we earlier mentioned *to mmara*, to which we now add its synonym, *mfom*, or *mfomdo*. Its basic meaning is to act in a disorderly manner, by committing a fault or transgressing a law. On the other hand, Akan society does not stop on the negative side. The Akan say *mfomdo kyerɛ nyimpa nyansa-pa, dɛm ntsi nyia ɔse ɔmmfom da no, ayew adze*—experience is the lesson we learn from our mistakes; therefore he who has never done wrong or claims never to have done wrong has missed an opportunity to learn.

Another metaphor is *mmusu*[25] (Twi; cf. Fante, *mbusu*), which literally means mischief, disaster, adversity. When Akan man says *bɔ mmusu*, he has caused mischief to come by an act. This metaphor focused on the evil that comes on the perpetrator of an evil deed. By an evil act a man comes under a curse. Evil deeds carry within themselves the seeds of self-destruction.

Even if we can find parallel terminology, we believe African theology should not attempt to match word for word all the terms for sin. Our concern should be more with translating the ideas. To that task we shall proceed presently.

The New Testament is united in its testimony that "all alike [Jew and Gentile, religious and nonreligious, Christian and non-Christian] have sinned, and are deprived of the divine splendour" (Rom. 3:23 NEB; cf. Rom. 3:9-20). Indeed, the First Letter of John goes further, that "if we claim to be sinless, we are self-deceived and strangers to the truth" (1:8 NEB). To be a man is to be a sinner, and to sin is a fact of human existence. And by the same token the New Testament affirms the universality of sin. Such a theology is not alien to most African societies. For example, the Gas of Ghana say *Gbomo adesa, gbomo adesa ni*—Oh man! the deeds of man. This is said when a man has caused some trouble or harm, and it affirms that it is expected of man to do harm. It asserts the unreliability of man. Man is by definition unreliable and therefore apt to cause harm to others and the society.

The Akan, our primary example, have several sayings that make the same point. The first is *ɔbra yɛ bɔ-na*—to be consistently good is difficult. This saying is used to advise young and inexperienced persons to watch their conduct. Again, the Akan say *suro onipa*—fear man. Man is to be feared because he is apt to cause harm to others through wicked acts. Apart from such sayings, several proverbs affirm the universality of sin and the inclination of man to evil. *Aboa kokosekyi se, Me nam wonndzi naaso nyimpa tsir mu yɛ sum ntsi motow me nkyirefua gu odupon nkɔn mu*—the vulture says, "Though I am not edible, yet I nurse my eggs in the branches of a high tree because man is hardly to be trusted." The point is that because man is by nature prone to evil, one should always be on his guard against him or expect the worst from him at any time. Another proverb says: *abowa adam se odompo ho bɔn na ɔnoɛ?*—faults in others make us forget our own shortcomings; otherwise the foul smelling ant should not tease a skunk of bad odor. The third proverb is *ber a w res n wudzifo bi nna "Emi-dze-mebɛyɛ-wu" ne dadze da ɔbo do*—the day the murderer dies on the gallows may be the day another impenitent criminal is deciding to commit murder. Men are so prone to sin that the experiences of others teaches them nothing.

The maxims and proverbs indicate that African tradition also affirms one of the points made by Christianity, namely that man is a sinner and is inclined to sin. With such maxims and proverbs we propose to teach that man is a sinner and cite biblical passages to reinforce them.

At this point we must say something about the idea of Original Sin, which in the New Testament is based on Romans 5:12: "It was through one man that sin entered the world, and through sin death, and thus death pervaded the whole human race, *inasmuch* as all men have sinned" (cf. I Cor. 15:21 NEB). This interpretation hinges on the Greek phrase *eph' hōi*, here rendered "inasmuch as." That phrase was taken by Augustine of Hippo in old Roman North Africa, following the great biblical scholar Origen of Alexandria, to be a reference to Adam, and therefore he translated it *in quo* (Latin)—in whom. Hence the translation: "it was through one man that sin entered the world . . . in whom all have sinned." In this translation there is an allusion to Genesis 2:17; 3:19, 6:23, and through that the idea that man has inherited the sin of Adam, so to speak.

However, that translation is inaccurate. In the view of modern scholarship *eph' hōi* is better translated "because." Thus "Adam is the symbol of that whole historical past which everyone inherits."[26] The passage does not speak of a solidarity in the consequences of the original transgression. Adam's sin had the gravest consequences for all men in the sense that it introduced death into the world by depriving man of glory and righteousness. Yet each man is guilty of his own faults. As the Apocalypse of Baruch puts it, "Adam is therefore not the cause, save only of his own soul, but each one of us has been the Adam of his own soul" (LIV. 19) The point is that there are some impulses which lead men to act contrary to the will of God. The technical term which the Jews used of this evil impulse is *Yetser-ha-ra'* (i.e., the root of evil or the evil impulse).[27] The impulse is not in itself evil, but it is evil in its effect when man has yielded himself to be impelled by it to consciously unlawful acts. Though to the first-century Jew, Adam was a historic personality, yet his story is also the story of the human situation.

So far as we have been able to discern, Akan society has no Adam mythology. But as we have seen above, the two ideas conveyed by the myth—the universality of sin, and man's inclination to sin—are already conveyed in maxims in Akan society. Our approach would be to use those maxims and sometimes to clinch the argument with biblical passages which are the charter documents of the church, which state fundamental principles.

The Adam myth highlights the solidarity of men not only in sin but also in the consequences of sin. First, sin brings about a separation between man and the spirit world. In the biblical faith man is chased out of the Garden. Akan man's version is expressed in the myth that when the old lady was rude to God, the latter moved further away, hence the recession of the firmament further away from man. Second, the consequence of sin, according to Genesis, is death. Similarly, the myth of the old lady also affirms death as the consequence of sin.

> Since they [i.e., the children of the old lady] could not get the one mortar required anywhere, their grandmother, that is the old woman, told her children saying, "Take one out from the bottom, and put it on the top to make them reach." So her children removed a single

one, and all rolled and fell to the ground, causing the death of many
people.

Death resulted from man's attempt to be on equal footing with God.
Third, one man's sin affects others in society. According to the
Akan, *edwane biako bɔ nsema a, ɔde saa benyinaa*—if one sheep
contracts craw-craw, it infects all the others in the fold.

Akan society, like the Christian church, affirms the solidarity of
man not only in sin but also in its consequences. We do not see
anything sacrosanct about the Adam myth itself, so we can use the
traditional phraseology and enrich it with the Adam mythology.

In the biblical myth of the Fall, Satan led Eve and Adam astray
(Gen. 3:58; cf. Rev. 12:9; I Thess. 2:18; I Cor. 2:8). Satan was
originally attorney-general in God's court (cf. book of Job). Later he
became the great adversary who was given to disrupting fellowship
between God and man by being the ultimate origin of evil.
Ephesians 6:12 gives the classic statement: "Our fight is not against
human foes, but against cosmic powers, against the authorities and
potentates of this dark world, against the superhuman forces of evil in
the heavens" (NEB). These cosmic powers are personal in the sense
that "they manifest themselves as beings of intellect and will, which
can speak and be spoken to. They are capable of purposeful activity.
But they are not always encountered as individuals. . . . [they] are
representatives of a collective principle. In them a collective spirit of
evil is at work."[28]

This personalization of the forces of evil is a difficult concept for
modern educated man, who dismisses it as nonsense. Whatever
modern man's attitude to it, the myth of Satan and demons
underlines the claim that man is in the grip of more than human
forces of evil,[29] leading to some sort of organized disobedience to the
will of God, an autonomous self-centeredness in opposition to God
and his power.

Once more there is a congruence of thinking between the biblical
and traditional Akan world views. Akan society also attributes evil to
personal forces of evil such as *esan* (Akan: bad luck), witches, and
sasabonsɛm. *Esan* and the witch are manifestations of Satan or
Sasabonsɛm. For according to the Akan, *sɛɔbayifo kɔ eyi a, ɔsoɛ
sasabons m*—when a witch attends a funeral, it is the devil who plays
him host. Thus in both world views, sin originates in personal forces
of evil. This most Africans should be comfortable with, though in

the more sophisticated sections of the society, some demythologizing will be necessary.

The solidarity of men in sin and the attribution of evil to personal forces of evil do not absolve man of individual and personal responsibility (cf. James 1:13-15). On this also, both the biblical and traditional African world views agree. Two Akan maxims should suffice to make the point. First, *Onyame mmpɛ bɔne nti na ɔmaa dine biako biako*—because God hates evil, he gave each one a name so as to identify the perpetrator of evil. In other words, each individual is responsible for his sin and accountable to God for it. The second saying is *ɔketeɛ nnkɔwe mako ma fifire nnfi ɔpankyerɛne*—it is the lizard that eats hot pepper that will get the burning sensation and not the frog which has not tasted it. Both sayings affirm individual and personal responsibility for sin, in spite of the ideas of corporate solidarity and demonic forces.

In the area of the individual and personal responsibility, the mainspring of evil in man is his own lust, i.e., any strong desire that holds a man—covetousness, improper sexual desire, craving for power or prominence (James 1:13-15), and so on. Again, Akan society has a similar idea: *Nyame a ɔbɔɔ me annyɛ me bɔn dɛ ɔtan a ɔwoo me na ɔdze fɛr hyɛɛ me nsa dɛ monkɔ hua mbra ma yɛndzi*—my Creator, God, did me no wrong; only hatred has so possessed me as to make me pine under disgrace by going to beg in order to be able to eat.[30] Another way of referring to lust is idolatry, not just the worship of wood and stone, but also the confusing of the creature with the Creator (Rom. 1:23).

The essence of sin is to seek to be as God, idolatry. This is the point of the biblical myth of man seeking to eat of the fruit of knowledge. *Homo Akanas* also sees sin as the desire to rub shoulders with God. This is the point of the myth of the old lady desiring to reach to the firmament. That is the rudeness which caused God to retreat further away from man. Idolatry, desire to rub shoulders with God, rudeness are all manifestations of egocentricity, which is the essence of sin. But for the same reason, Akan society emphasizes the communal nature of sin.

Earlier it was said that *homo Akanus'* ontology is *cognatus ergo sum*. Consequently, his ethics is community oriented, or, if you like, it emphasizes the horizontal dimension of morality. *Sɛ aburo dua ne ho a, ɔte tɔ*—if corn seeks to plant itself, it falls and dies. Egocentricity is wicked and self-defeating and as such is deprecated.

Or again, the Akan say *benkum dware nifa, na nifa dware benkum*—the left hand washes the right, and vice versa. This proverb highlights the need for reciprocity as well as a man's obligations to other members of the society. Again, *ber a irutwa sa ekotu ninsin no nna iritu obi so ne ninsin gu*—the way you adopt to achieve something may be the means to endanger another man's chance.

If the ontology is *cognatus ergo sum*, then one man's evil reflects on others in the society: *abɛ biako na esɛe nsa*—one palm tree (among many) can spoil the taste of the palm wine. One bad member of a society may ruin the reputation of the society with his bad conduct. Consequently, a woman may not be given in marriage because of the tarnished reputation of a leading member of the family. On the other hand, the good of a man may reflect on others: *onipa yɛ yiyɛ a, ɔyɛ gyaw ne mma*—if a man is good, his children benefit by it after his death. The descendants of a good man may reap the fruits of his goodness. This saying is well suited to capture the idea that believers in Christ may benefit from the merits of the good works of Christ.

Again the biblical faith and Akan society agree that evil cannot escape unpunished. The Akan say *abɔfra bɔ mmusu akrona, ɔfa mu anum*—if a child commits nine crimes, he bears the punishment for five, the remaining four being presumably borne by the family. In other words, the results of a man's misdeeds are borne not by the man alone, but by the man himself and his family. Again, he says *sɛ nyimpa bɔhwe ase a, nna ofi bɔn nkakraba; dza ɔdze hɛn hwe famu no nnyɛ akoko bi, na nkukuw a*—it is not the mountains but the small stumps of sin in life's way that cause our downfall. Sin, however small, carries its own punishment, sooner or later. Finally, he also says, *wodi ntorɔ a, woberɛ*—you suffer if you tell lies. There is no rest for the liar.

It is now time to draw the threads together. Sin (Akan, *bɔne*) is not altogether a new idea in Akan society. It is a deed or a thought which affects the good relations with the spirit-world. One difference at this stage is that whereas in Christianity it is only God who is affected, in traditional society there are also the gods and ancestors. But that is because God is seen as such a big king that his agents, the ancestors and gods, act *in loco Dei* and *pro Deo*. An African theology has two options before us: to deemphasize the gods and ancestors or to deny entirely the role of the gods. My approach is the former of the two: sin is the violation of the demands of the King of heaven, whose courtiers, the gods and ancestors, the part of the clan gone ahead, are outraged by man's disobedience.

At this point, some of the teaching of St. Anselm comes in handy.[31] God as the great King is omnipotent; he has immediate power over man and even Satan. We would ourselves add the entire spirit-world. By sin both man and Satan attempt to escape from God and thereby to rob him of his power over them, albeit in vain. The essence of sin, therefore, is to rob God of the honor due to him as the great King; it is to owe God what is his due, namely, respect, obedience, and love. It is to be rude like the old lady in the Akan myth.

African theology's exposition of sin must emphasize the horizontal aspect of sin. If *homo Africanus'* ontology is *cognatus ergo sum* and the extended family is the *summum bonum*, motivation and conduct are expected to be directed to that end.[32] Sin, therefore, is any act which does not contribute to the welfare and continuance of the family and detracts from the *sensus communis*. Sin is the word or deed which putrefies fellowship in one family. Our new emphasis would be to go beyond the extended family to all human beings as children of God's family.

African theology, through the maxims and proverbs quoted above, must affirm the universality of sin and the individual responsibility for sin, even if also evil may be attributed to personal forces of evil.[33] The post-Copernican age tends to exorcize the universe of the supernatural. Today there are signs that the pendulum is swinging back to the quest after the supernatural and the numinous. We believe this to be the significance of the popularity of transcendental meditation and the guru movements. In Africa, witchcraft beliefs continue to hold their ground and to some extent account for the popularity of the "spiritual" churches, which are sometimes also called "witchcraft eradication movements" because that appears to be a major concern and preoccupation. So with no apology one can speak of sin as captivity by the forces of evil—*sasabonsɛm* or *ayɛn* (witchcraft).

The reference to witchcraft leads us to the next point. Witchcraft is the Akan's myth to express the tensions within the kinship group and it is evidence of man's need to be loved. So witchcraft is the opposite of *adɔyɛ*, love, which in the biblical faith is the foremost characteristic of God as well as that of his devotees. For the moment our interest is to claim that sin is the denial of *adɔyɛ*. That also is the dynamo of Akan society; for the Akan says *Adiama ne adiama ne agoru*—good fellowship is sharing good things with your friends. Stealing is a denial of *adɔyɛ*. Sexual sins are wrong not in their sexuality but in the fact that the dangerous intensity of the act is channeled against the proper structure of the family and becomes an attack on its members. Consequently, when a girl is caught in illicit sex, it is said that the man *ruku ɔbaa no egya ne sunsum*—he is killing the soul of the girl's father. Sin has psychic effect on another person. The material act is not the most important; sin is the attitude of heart and mind which spoils the life force of another, especially the life force of the family, the dynamo of which is *adɔyɛ*.

The biblical faith goes beyond the denunciation of man as a sinner to offer him the hope of salvation through faith in Jesus Christ. That, as we saw above, has its adumbration in the maxim *onipa yɛ yiyɛ a, ɔyɛ gyaw ne mma*—if a man (e.g., Jesus) is good, his children benefit by it after his death. We call this an adumbration of the Christian teaching because it lacks the content of vicarious suffering. But that is the subject for a study of the atonement. Be that as it may, the way out of sin is *adɔyɛ*, the ethic of love. That seems to us to be the heart of the teaching with regard to sin in an African theology. That which does not conform to the standard of *adɔyɛ* is sin because it sunders the cohesion of the society by destroying the personality of both victim and perpetrator and in the process challenges the honor, integrity, and dignity of the great King, God.

VII

Christian Marriage in Africa

According to the Population Census of 1960,[1] the religious composition of Ghana is as follow:

Christians 42.8%
     Roman Catholics 13.4%
     Methodists 10.3%
     Presbyterians 9.9%
     Anglicans 2.6%
     Others 6.6%

Adherents of African Traditional Religions 38.2%
Muslim 12%
No Religion 7%

These figures show that for about 93 percent of the population of Ghana, religion of one form or other has some importance and significance. The figures also indicate that religiously speaking, at any rate, Ghana is pluralistic, with Christianity, African traditional religions, and Islam as the most important and major religions. Consequently, it should occasion no surprise that there are at least three types of marriages in Ghana: (a) native customary marriage; (b) ordinance marriage, which refers to what is contracted either in church or at the registrar's offices; and (c) Muslim marriage. All of these have legal standing in the laws of the land, although, as we shall see later, there is a tendency in some circles to accord the ordinance marriage greater respect than the others.[2] Furthermore, these three major religions have lived alongside one another and not in isolation. Indeed, it may even be argued that they have influenced one another. Thus quite a few Ghanians who claim to be Christian have also contracted polygamous marriages, which in principle are unacceptable to Christians. Or again, many a Christian first goes through the motions stipulated for marriages under customary law and then moves on to marriage under the Ordinance, such as the Christian rite.

It is of moment that the church clarifies for herself how Christianity and traditional religion and custom can fruitfully live alongside each other, whether in friendship or in hostility or in a syncretistic relationship. This, though said specifically of Ghana, is true in varying degrees of other African countries also.

In the rest of Black Africa, as in Ghana, marriage remains a key problem for the church. According to the 1960 Population Census Post-Enumeration Survey, 91 percent of all females and 65 percent of all males aged fifteen and over were married, divorced, or widowed. That is, nine out of every ten adult women and seven out of every ten adult men had married at least once. In other words, marriage is the norm. Indeed, modern African societies, like traditional African societies, do not take kindly to the marriageable young man or woman who does not marry. They tend to treat him or her as a half citizen. What has the Christian church to say to African man for whom marriage is the norm and a must?

It appears the church has not convinced African man on this matter of marriage. That appears to be the implication of the fact that most Christians are said to live in sin because their marriages fall short of the standard set by the church or are in some technical deviation. For example, in 1960, 87.6 percent of the Roman Catholic married men of Ghana were not "lawfully married" because they had not contracted ordinance marriages. Of the Roman Catholic females, 88.3 percent were not "lawfully married."[3] In all denominations, many Christians have been barred from the Lord's Supper because their marriages do not measure up to the standards of the church. It is not unusual to find an active and practicing churchman who has a concubine[4] in addition to his wife; or, worse still, in addition to his regular wife has a lover or paramour who for all practical purposes is his wife even though the relationship has not been sanctioned by the parents of either party. The words of the Rt. Rev. John Orfeur Aglionby, late Bishop of the Anglican diocese of Accra, written in 1939, are, by and large, true even now: "There is no doubt that the loss among our communicants is most frequently due to their breaking of the marriage law of the Church; the man takes to himself another wife, or a woman becomes one of several wives of another man."[5]

To my mind the church's attitude to customary marriages has been characterized by arrogance and supercilious conceit. She does not appear to be impressed with the fact that African countries such as Ghana and Nigeria are pluralistic societes. Consequently, she tends to behave as though her viewpoint is the last and incontrovertible word, which has to be taken without question or be damned. Let me illustrate this point.

In the early 1960s, the administration of Mr. Kwame Nkrumah, the first Prime Minister of Ghana, issued a Government White Paper on the subject of marriage.[6] It pleaded for the recongition "of those of our customs and usages, which are not contrary to the Natural Law and Natural Morality." It pleaded for the registration of one wife, even though there may be other wives. Again, it argued for the recognition of divorce, but only after several attempts by the two families to reconcile the couple have failed. Finally, it also emphasized that no minister of religion would be compelled to perform any marriage service that was contrary to the tenets of his faith and confession.

The combined opposition of the church and other groups in the country forced the government to withdraw the White Paper. In fact, the issue was never again raised. But if the matter was dropped and seemed to die, it was no real victory for the church; rather it was a catastrophe, because in practice avowed churchmen have not lived up to the standards of the church. To be sure, I myself cannot accept all the details of the White Paper's provisions. For example, I cannot accept the registration of one wife because it treats others as second-class wives. Why may one's sister not be the first wife who is registered and thus have all the prestige and security that goes with it? Nevertheless, one is grateful for the White Paper because at the very least the government by it showed that it was aware that there was a problem about marriage which caused great pain and anguish to men and women and which needed to be solved. The church for her part made a lot of noise and offered no solution, failing to show sensitivity to people's problems. It still is an open question as to how the church can satisfy the African mind on the issue of marriage.

In African societies life is marked by crisis points, by *rites de passage*. Marriage stands with birth, puberty, and death as a rite of passage. Each crisis point partakes of a religious nature because in traditional society, life is based on the religious postulate.[7] Furthermore, since African man's ontology is *cognatus ergo sum*, these rites have a communal dimension in the sense that they involve the extended family and incorporate the minors into the extended family. The rite of marriage thus becomes a matter of public recognition and indicates that the society is interested in protecting that alliance of families and the terms under which it recognizes and protects the alliance. The religious and communal understanding of these rites of passage carries with it obligations and rights within the nuclear and extended family.

It is by design that I have underlined the idea that marriage is a *rite de passage* because I wish to draw two conclusions. First, since the rite is a manifestation of the ontology *cognatus ergo sum*, the rite, among other things, gives each member a feeling or sense of belonging and continuity. Therefore, an African cannot be expected to leave his ancestral tradition without good and convincing reasons. The mere pontification of the church is not enough to effect a change of heart and direction.

Second, because marriage is a *rite de passage* like birth, puberty, and death, I am displeased with the expression "Christian marriage." For that description has encouraged arrogance among Christians, talking as if marriage under the ordinance alone is the right or proper marriage. It has encouraged the situation in which marriage according to the traditional African custom is at the best tolerated and is often not respected. I believe such attitudes are mistakes. For as long as the stipulated motions have been fulfilled, there is a valid and respectable marriage. In any case, just as one does not normally talk of "a Christian birth" or "a Christian puberty" or "a Christian death," one is reluctant to speak of "Christian marriage."

On the other hand, one also understands that there is a Christian interpretation and understanding of marriage, just as there is a Christian interpretation and understanding of birth, puberty, and death. For that reason a Christian is obliged to bring his marriage, whether "contracted" under the ordinance or under customary law, into the purview of his religion, because he is obliged to present his whole life "a living sacrifice, holy and acceptable to God" (Rom. 12:1 RSV). In practical terms it means that the marriage should be informed by the Christian ethic of selfless and self-sacrificing devotion to the partner. In other words, in the matrimonial home itself there should be selfless and self-sacrificing service and devotion to the nuclear family. The wedding service itself is only the beginning of a marital life. It is the occasion for the public recognition of the union and for the declaration of the terms of that recognition.

In fairness to Christianity, let us put on record that although the tendency was toward a negative attitude to the customary marriages, individual church leaders took an enlightened view from time to time. Thus, for example, the Rt. Rev. Mowbray Stephen O'Rorke, Anglican Bishop of Accra (1913–1923), moved in the right direction when he counseled the recognition of customary marriages but with two provisos: the consent of the parties before witnesses and a promise of a lifelong and exclusive association. [8]

Let us dwell a little on the wedding ceremony itself. In Africa, which has a great love for pomp, pageantry, and ceremony, a good deal of stress is put on the wedding ceremony, and the Christian qualities of the matrimonial home are often forgotten. Partly as a result of the emphasis on the wedding, marriages in church have tended to be expensive, with much money being spent on expensive dress and liquor for that occasion. Consequently, the question is often asked, Is it necessary to have a church wedding? And if so, what form should it take? The church should not be blamed for people's inability and failure to cut their coats according to their pockets. There is nothing Christian about the trousseau, nor does the church require it for a valid marriage.

As was said above, a Christian is obliged to bring his whole life into the purview of his religion. Therefore, an important occasion like a wedding, which marks a turning point in the life of a couple, must also be brought into the purview of their religion, their Christian profession, to be precise. Second, since the biblical faith rejects the idea of the individual, isolated Christian because belonging to the church is a *sine qua non* of being in Christ, it follows that the community of the faithful is to be involved as the witness of that change of marital status. The couple at the wedding should make their vows or covenant before God and the people of God. This should not be a difficult concept. For already in traditional society, marriage is between two families. Thus in our Christian context we shall be broadening the family from the blood group to the fellowship of believers in Christ. Again, because the marriage is more than a covenant between a couple or even between the two extended families, the church and the state prescribe the terms under which they recognize and protect the marriage. In a sense, the wedding ceremony is a dramatization of the coming together of the couple by a covenant, and that with the fellowship of believers and God.[9] The priest or minister represents the people to give a Christian witness to the union of the couple and of both families. The priest or minister cannot make or unmake the marriage. For in the wisdom of the church, the efficacy of any sacrament does not depend on the worthiness of the priest but the one for whose sake (i.e. Christ or God) the sacrament was made.[10] It is the couple who either make or unmake the marriage; it is the couple who openly make their covenant to be a new kindred. The couple themselves are the minister of the sacrament.

One last comment on the wedding rite: as of now, we have at least two parallel rites in Africa, the Christian and the traditional. The two appear to be treated as though they were in watertight compartments. One could wish that the two would be integrated. Ideally one would suggest that when the two families sit together to pursue the traditional rites of marriage in the family house of the girl, the specifically Christian vows, e.g., the promise of a lifelong and exclusive association, should be introduced at that point.

We have earlier stressed the validity and respectability of traditional African marriage. But this does not mean every aspect of it is acceptable to Christians. This is where we now turn to the genuinely problematic areas in the dialogue between Christianity and African custom on the subject of marriage.

The Christian church's understanding of marriage is that of a union between husband and wife. In biblical language they become "one flesh." Behind that kind of language and thinking stands the story of the creation of Eve from Adam, as it is told by Genesis 2. The story elucidates by comparison "the agelong urgency of the sexes for one another, which is only appeased when it becomes 'one flesh' in a child; for the woman was taken from the man, and they must in consequence come together again."[11] One aspect of it is well expressed by the Hebrew word *yada'*—to know. That is more than a mere process of intellect; it is rather knowledge of all things about the other partner and the attainment of mastery over all things and secrets of the other partner.

For many an African the idea and practice of "one flesh" is difficult. Here I will mention two questions often asked. The first is, Is it possible for two different persons with different backgrounds, different mentalities, different mental equipment, and different development and capacities to come together to be one flesh? To my mind this is not a peculiarly African problem. Properly understood, they do not lose their individuality; they are a unit or a unity in a harmonious relationship to be the basic unit for a household and family. They are one kindred. That means that in the matrimonial home they cannot go their several ways. They are to be in selfless and self-sacrificing devotion to each other and to their children. That is why in the wedding service they vow "to have and to hold, for better or for worse, for richer or for poorer, in sickness or in health, till death us do part."

The second problem, the more difficult one, relates to African man's ontology that *cognatus ergo sum*, namely that he finds the fullest meaning of his existence in the extended family to which he is related by blood. Consequently, the idea of "one flesh" is constantly put to the test by the extended family system. Akan society was aware of the obligations of the extended family to the new unit. For according to an Akan proverb, *Awarsɔ na awargu ne fabi gyina nsewnom do*—the success or failure of a marriage to some extent depends on the attitudes of the parents-in-law. This to my mind is plain common sense. However, ever so often the members of the extended family intrude into the nuclear family, especially if the man is the main breadwinner of his family. On the other hand, one of the aims of a female in marriage in traditional society is economic: she seeks to acquire property through marriage as an investment for the security of her matrimonial relations in the society. The result is that quite often the wives do not contribute financially to their matrimonial home, leaving that aspect to the man. Thus the extended family system, again and again and in diverse manners, puts the one flesh idea to the test, and that under great stress.

I do not believe that the one-flesh idea is to be equated with the European nuclear family. After all, the biblical world which preached one flesh also had the extended family. To my mind the real issue is to keep the right balance between one's obligations to the nuclear family and his obligations to the extended family. This means a man cannot prefer his nephews to his own children; nor can it be right that a wife should feel that her financial obligations are primarily to her relatives.

The union is, in the Christian tradition, meant to be permanent, i.e., for the whole life. Hence the phrase in the matrimonial vows "till death us do part." In the biblical tradition, marriage was originally—i.e., in the primordial will of God—intended to be indissoluble (Mark: 10:2-12; cf. Matt. 19:3-4; I Cor. 7:10; cf. Gen. 1:27; 2:24). Consequently, divorce is disapproved in principle.

Divorce is regarded by Jesus as a concession to human weakness and hardness of heart. The discussion takes off from Deuteronomy 24:1, which in its original context is not about divorce in general. That passage assumes the right of divorce. But divorce must be attested by a properly formulated legal document (Hebrew, *Get*) which must be formally served on the wife and executed by a formal sending out of the woman. Originally too, only men had the right to divorce. But late Judaism allowed women to initiate divorce proceedings on a few specified grounds: the man being a leper suffering polypus, or being engaged in a repulsive trade.[12] However Deuteronomy 24:1, properly speaking, concerns the impossibility of remarrying a woman who has been separated from her husband once already. In New Testament times the grounds for divorce were debated between the schools of Rabbi Hillel and Rabbi Shammai. The former was more lax than the latter. For on the basis of the phrase *'erwath dabhar*—for some uncleanness (Deut. 24:1)—Hillel approved divorce for anything the husband disapproved about his wife, including burning the food. On the other hand, the stricter school of Shammai approved divorce for only what was morally shameful, especially unchastity.[13] The discussion of divorce in Matthew 5:32 and 19:9 appears to make Jesus grant divorce for unchastity (Greek, *porneia*), and therefore according to the Shammai tradition. Whether the *porneia* exception of Matthew 5:32 and 19:9 is authentically from Jesus need not detain us here or affect the basic argument that divorce with or without cause is a departure from the Christian norm.

That marriage should be lifelong and indissoluble is again different from traditional African thinking on the subject. To the traditional African, marriage is a social question, even if its problems are solved with religious belief and conception. They feel that God has given people the free will either to come together or to stay apart. Therefore, divorce is neither sacrilegious nor antisocial. As a proverb puts it, *aware yɛ yɛnko, ɔŋnyɛ abusua*—marriage is friendship and not a family. Consequently, if the two felt the friendship could not continue for any reason or reasons—e.g., impotence, sterility, sexual neglect of the wife—they went their several ways without any sense of sin. Indeed, as M. Fortes has suggested, the kinship ties of a matrimonial society make for divorce because the father apparently has no legal authority over his children nor can he claim custody of the children as a right. Therefore, divorce makes no change in the domestic circumstances and economic situation of the woman. Divorce affects neither her jural status nor that of her children. Obviously to denounce divorce as sin in such a society is to fail to communicate and acquit oneself creditably.

In Ghana, divorce appears to be a serious problem. In 1960 the Post Enumeration Survey revealed the rate of divorce as follows:

I. Ghana as a Whole (Christian and non-Christian

	men	5.2%
	women	7.2%
Western region:	men	6.1%
	women	9.9%
Greater Accra:	men	3.8%
	women	6.3%
Eastern Region:	men	6 %
	women	9.5%
Volta Region:	men	4.3%
	women	4.6%
Ashanti Region:	men	5.9%
	women	10.6%
Brong-Ahafo Region:	men	5.7%
	women	8.8%
Northern Region:	men	4 %
	women	1.5%

II. Divorcees Among Christian Population of Ghana

men	4.27%
women	9.87%

III. Divorce Cases Filed at Accra High Court, 1970–75

1970	52
1971	47
1972	101
1973	107
1974	99
1975	82
Total	488

It appears the rate of remarriage after divorce is high.[14]

On the face of it, there can be no bridging of the gulf between Christianity and African custom on the subject of the lifelong and indissoluble nature of marriage. To my mind it should not be too difficult to preach lifelong marriage for two reasons. First, as a matter of fact and sober history, many Africans outside the Christian tradition—in fact the majority—have lifelong marriages. The second reason is the increasingly harsh cost of living, which makes marriage a very expensive affair. The trickier idea is the indissolubility of marriage which is definitely and unequivocally against African tradition. To this problem let us address ourselves.

First, let us admit that the churches have tended to be legalistic in their enforcement of the indissolubility principle. Divorce is not the worst sin, even if we do not wish to condone it. The church will be better advised to take seriously the circumstances leading to the break-up of the marriage. So let us, second, turn to the question of the purpose of marriage.

In the Christian tradition, marriage is for three things: procreation, comfort and companionship, and "that the natural instincts and affections planted by God, should be hallowed and directed aright."[15] The third reason finds biblical support in I Corinthians 7:9f, where Paul counsels the Corinthians to marry rather than be consumed by passion. The second reason, comfort and companionship, finds its basis in the creation of Eve to be a helpmeet of Adam. The first reason, procreation, is an aspect of the one-flesh idea we discussed above (cf. Tobit 8:7).

I do not see that any of these three aims is particularly objectionable to the Akan. And we must at this point examine what the aim of marriage is in traditional society.

Akan woman is expected to limit her activities to hearth and home, kitchen, and nursery. This statement of the role of the female in traditional society summarizes the aims of marriage. First, it was for procreation. Marriage and procreation are the means of continuing the family, which consists of the living, the dead, and the unborn. Consequently, childlessness was considered a great disaster not only for the individual but also for the clan. Even to have only one child is a disaster, though slightly better than childlessness. A woman with just one child is stigmatized as *sebɔ*—the leopardess, thereby denying her normal human qualities. Consequently, childlessness and having only one child often lead either to concubinage to prove one's virility and to increase the clan, or to divorce. Normally divorce is allowed only after all efforts at reconciliation have failed. But in the case of impotence, particularly in men, no attempt is made at reconciliation. If the woman is to blame for the lack of children, then the man may marry a second wife, but with the approval of the wife. All these comments serve to underline that marriage for the Akan man is for procreation. According to the Akan proverb, *basia kwasea na sɛ ɔkɔ awar a, ɔwo Badu*—a serviceable wife is often blessed with the birth of a tenth child.

To my mind, the church cannot ultimately accept divorce on the grounds of childlessness or for having only one child. That seems to me immoral because it amounts to using the wife as a means to an end rather than seeing her as an end in herself. Besides, it amounts to doing unto another what he may not like done to him. For if the woman were to decide to leave the man for his impotence, he would not like it. And, indeed, there have been many suicides among men in African societies because of alleged impotence. The attitude that condones this is a denial of the Christian meaning of love. Pointing out the basic issues at stake to the one bent on divorce because of childlessness, should strike a cord in the heart of *homo Akanus* because of the proverb, *abaa a wɔdze bɔ Takyi, wɔdze bɔ Baah*—the rod used on Takyi is sure to be used on Baah as well. Thus African tradition, like Christianity, pleads for the uniform application of the principle. But one recognizes also that men are not always consistent. In any case, one suffering a bad toothache is in no mood for explanations but just wants the problem solved. So too, one whose marriage is in a difficulty because of childlessness will be in no mood for theories and explanations of principles. So part of the problem is getting the willingness even to listen.

A second reason for marriage in traditional society is investment.

But the nature of the investment is not the same for the man as for the woman. For the man it is the investment of having someone to look after the home. Consequently, for him there is stress on the cooking. The Akan say *basia ennsua adze yε na ɔkɔ awar a, wɔdze no nkwan gu bɔdambɔ mu kyerε aman*—a young lady who does not learn to cook and keep house shall after marriage have her soup exhibited to the general public, as evidence of her incompetence at housekeeping. And that will be grounds for divorce. So for the man, the investment of marriage is to have a keeper of the home.

On the other hand, the woman's security is elsewhere, and that in two ways. First, the Akan say *wo dan wo na kaw a, wokɔto w'egya de*[16]—a wife's debts and liabilities belong to the husband. Thus a wife invests in marriage in the sense that her relationship to the husband should help improve the financial circumstances of the maternal side. For women, marriage is an investment in yet another sense: *basia tse dε borɔdzewa; banyin dze eburow man a*—in a matrilineal society, a woman is to be compared to a banana tree which multiplies itself, and man is a cornstalk which stands alone. In a matrilineal society, marriage is an investment because it ensures the continuity of the woman's line and family.

To our mind the idea of investment is not necessarily immoral, even though it can be abused. Our only concern here is to emphasize the need for the right balance between obligations to the nuclear family and those to the extended family.

A third reason for marriage in traditional society is the need for spiritual protection which is sustained only in the male of the society. The male is the source of the woman's spiritual protection. At this point we draw attention to the discussion on *sunsum* and *ntorɔ* in chapter 3. The Akan say *Kotokurenkyi, Kotokurenkyi ase nye dε 'akontan so y busuanyi*—a brother-in-law is also a member of the matrilineal extended family through whom the family members increase. By marriage he belongs to the family of the wife. Again *homo Akanus* says *basia yε ture mu nhyiren a, okun so nye no ho ban*—woman is a flower in the garden; her husband the fence around it. Obviously the husband protects the wife. And this may be Akan man's version of comfort and companionship of marriage. There is nothing particularly un-Christian about it.

On balance, therefore, the Christian and traditional Akan marriage aims are complementary and travel much the same way and direction. The crucial thing is for the churches to show sensitivity to the hopes and fears of the Africans.

One of the areas of African man's hopes and fears is the issue of childlessness, to which we now return. We suggested above that fertility and procreativity, so to speak, are the key to a man's authentic existence.[17] So childlessness is almost an intractable problem. Earlier one line of counter-argument was suggested, i.e., an appeal to the innate sense of fair play. To that we now wish to add a second argument: perhaps the church could use the occasion to affirm that childlessness too may be a part of God's plan for the couple. The Akan say *awo yɛ Onyame akyedze*—birth is the gift of God. We propose to use this determinism and predestinarian thinking of traditional society to test the depth and sincerity of a man's faith in God as the ground of his being. On the other hand, one recognizes a problem with regard to this argument. For modern science is convincing that incompatible blood grouping can be the cause of infertility. And so, some may wish to interpret their childlessness as the punishment of God for their careless or even wrong choice of a partner. To that argument we have no answer that is ultimately convincing. At the end of the day, one can only be in the spirit of Job that only God is his own interpreter and the problem of childlessness is a mystery to live with. To be able to pull through the condition of childlessness in a society which considers it a disaster requires a leap of faith which only God himself can make possible.

Before leaving the subject of the indissolubility of marriage, let us recall that the biblical faith is aware of a fact of life—that the marriage bond is not readily destroyed or wiped out, not even when a court has granted a *decree Nisi*. For sexual union involves knowing the other partner thoroughly as to his or her secrets which he or she does not readily share with anyone who is not really intimate. This, as we saw above, the Hebrews described with *yada'*—to know all things and attain the mastery over all things and secrets. That kind of knowledge and its accompanying feelings do not easily get lost. That is why it is possible for divorced persons to long for each other, to feel the pain of separation, and to enter into sexual union despite a *decree Nisi*.

In the Pauline letters there is another type of dissolution of marriage which is the separation without divorce (I Cor. 7:11). That also is disapproved in principle. But it appears to be the lesser of evils:

on the one hand, a full divorce, and, on the other hand, living in the agony of a broken marriage and home. All the same, separation without divorce is also a deviation from the norm. In fact I believe it is a matter of semantics to draw a distinction between divorce and separation. And a statement of no divorce or separation as the norm for a Christian is a nonnegotiable aspect of African theology, though individual cases may be considered on their own merits. Under no circumstances must the norm be confused with the concession and vice versa.

So far we have looked at the divorce issue from the standpoint of the couple themselves. That is not all. The children too must be considered. The emotional influence of divorces on the infant dependents may stifle the children's progress to marriage. Further, in a modern African home,[18] a divorce may deprive the child of the father as a model from whom he or she learns to play his or her own adult roles.

A last word on divorce. The church has often shown legalism on the issue of marriage, particularly when it comes to divorce. In our efforts to proclaim the Christian message with regard to marriage to *homo Africanus*, we propose to affirm that in principle divorce is unacceptable. But we propose to balance it with a careful consideration of the merits of each case. For in Christian ethics there is such a thing as the lesser of two evils or the greater good. When we see that the marriage has broken down beyond repair and when all exhaustive attempts at repair have failed, then it would be useless, nay, hypocritical and immoral, pretending that it has not broken down. It would also be self-deception. Further, we shall seek the path of the lesser of two evils: the first being to compel the couple to live together under the same roof, worrying the soul out of each other, leading to drunkenness, drug-taking, or possible murder, not to mention the mental torture and agony. Drunkenness, for example, is often symptomatic of the moral degradation of a society or individual who is sinking ever deeper into a state of chronic alcoholic poisoning. Many resort to it in a feeling of impotence, discontent, and disillusionment. The church owes such people pastoral concern and care rather than downright and careless condemnation. The other evil is to allow the Christian to break the Christian norm of indissolubility and permanence of marriage in these given circumstances. Surely the latter of the two is the better of the two alternatives, or the lesser of the two evils. So under certain circumstances, after much prayer and thought, we may countenance divorce. But when we do this, we shall also leave none in any doubt that the divorce is a special concession to them in their given circumstances when the marriage has hopelessly broken down, and against our Christian norm. The law should be tempered with mercy and sensitivity. For the breakdown of marriage is a tragedy not only for the couple and their families but also for the Christian community and witness. And tragedy must be met with sympathy as well as justice. This approach is consistent with the teaching and practice of Jesus, for whom man was and is the measure of the sabbath and the law, and therefore who denied the absolute claims of sanctified traditions.

Christian marriage is meant to be a permanent and exclusive union between a man and his wife, and that for life. This condition has been technically known as monogamy. On the other hand, customary marriage tended to be polygynous, i.e., a man *tended* to have more than one wife.[19] Polygyny was and is a tendency but is not of the essence of African traditional practice. Not only have there been many non-Christian Africans who have had monogamous marriages—indeed, it might well be that there are many more monogamists than polygynists—but there are indications that traditional society was not too pleased with polygyny. Suffice it here to outline some five sayings and maxims of Akan society to substantiate it:

(a) *Awar dodow ma banyin tɛkyerɛma yɛ nta*—polygyny makes a husband a double-tongued man.[20] There is danger in polygyny—it affects one's integrity.

(b) *Mmae dodow kunu yare a, ɔkɔm na ekum no*—if a polygynist is taken ill, he is starved to death because each wife thinks another wife will cook for him. In other words, everybody's business is nobody's business. A polygynist falls between two stools. There is no real security in polygyny.

(c) *Ayere dodow yɛ ohia na enyɛ hwee*—polygyny is nothing but poverty. Polygyny imposes financial strain on every husband.

(d) *Wopɛ akasakasa a, na woware yerenom bebrebe*—if you wish to be frequently disturbed with quarrels, then you marry several wives. In other words, there is no peace and calm in polygyny.

(e) *Wopata adadesan abien hye gya mu a, biako hyew*—if you

have two bars of iron in the fire, one gets burnt. One cannot
satisfy all parties in polygynous marriage because some are
bound to be shortchanged.

From the five proverbs quoted above, it is obvious that native
traditional wisdom saw real dangers in polygyny: (a) there was no real
security and peace in a polygynous marriage; (b) polygyny puts the
integrity and honesty of the man under strain; (c) it puts the man
under a financial strain and burden; and (d) it cannot be fair to all the
parties. So even if quite a few traditionalists contracted polygyny,
that is far from saying that polygyny was considered the ideal for
society. Why, then, did and do men contract polygyny?

First, polygyny was undertaken to satisfy the desire for children in
the family to continue the family tradition. Childlessness and
infertility are the number one cause of polygyny. Here we draw
attention to what was said above about childlessness as a factor in
divorce cases. That desire for children is often accompanied, nay
aggravated, by strong pressures from society and one's immediate
kith and kin. All too often, when there has been no issue within two
years of marriage, relations begin to drop hints or even maneuver to
have a girl of their choice arrive at the scene. Once a relation turned
up at the house of a couple who had been married for two years with
a cat which was solemnly left behind. That was a parabolic acting out
of the need for companions in children. It requires great courage and
calmness of head to resist that kind of pressure.

Second, traditionally and to some extent even today, polygyny has
come about for economic reasons. In a simple society with a simple
economy, if any, a man was well helped by his farm or fishing boat.
The more hands one had to whom he did not have to pay out wages,
the better it was for the man. Their wants were taken care of in a
communalistic kind of life, and they for their part worked to
contribute to the communal fund. Therefore, many children and
several wives were an economic asset.

Third, the desire for male children and heirs propelled people into
polygyny. Mention has been made earlier of the desire to acquire
spiritual protection sustained only in the male of the society.
Further, since girls soon marry off into other families, it is a concern
to have a male to retain the family name. Consequently, if there
have been only girls from a marriage, there is a tendency to seek
fortunes elsewhere if the assumption is that the sex of the children is
the wife's fault. Hence a polygynous relationship.

Finally, polygyny was a sort of family planning. In traditional societies, as soon as a woman became pregnant, she went off to the care of her parents. And she did not return till she was ready to assume full duties and responsibilities as a housewife. Altogether she would be away for at least two years, or more often nearer three to four years, because the weaning of the child was the indication that she was ready to resume her full role as a housewife. From that point of view there is family planning. But since nature abhors a vacuum, a second wife comes in to do what the first wife should be doing. And, of course, by the time the first wife is ready to return to her role as housewife, the second wife will be ready to go on maternity leave. Viewed from the standpoint of each wife, the polygynous marriage aids family planning.

The reasons for polygyny outlined above are not the only reasons. But these are not frivolous; they are respectable reasons, even if they do not appeal to us personally. Nor is the polygynous relationship a unilateral decision by the man. He contracts a second marriage with the full permission of the first wife and sometimes at the instigation of the first wife. And the second wife comes in with the clear understanding that she is there to help the first wife. In the cultural ethos it is not immoral, nor is it an attempt to cheat. So it is useless for Christians to devote so much time and energy denouncing polygyny as a wicked institution. So what should the church do about polygyny?

There are two separate issues here: (a) what should the church do with the polygynist who wishes to be a member of the church? (b) What should the church do with a member of the church who decides to be a polygynist? The first of the two questions is perhaps the easier of the two with which to deal. We affirm unequivocally that the church is in principle opposed to polygyny. On the other hand, it is also desirable for people to come into the church, because we have a mission to make disciples of the whole world, including even the polygynist. At the same time, the polygynist is also in a valid union with the other women, having gone through the stipulated motions of the society. Therefore, our approach to the polygynist should be along the following lines: You are already in a valid fellowship and relationship with more than one wife. You did this in good faith before you heard the Christian standard and style. To ask you to put away all your wives except one would be to cause hardship and pain to them, leaving them as "damaged goods," so to speak, whom none may look at again. It would be to consign them to a painful, uncertain future, and that would be evil. We receive you by baptism and confirmation into the fellowship of Christians, knowing fully well that you are a polygynist. In adopting this position, we are rejecting the advice of the Lambeth Conference of 1888 that polygynists should not be accepted into the church.[21] To us that advice is misguided and arrogant and legalistic. It also denies the charge to make converts of all nations, including even outcasts. Our approach is to choose between the lesser of two evils: the lesser evil being to break the church's norm of monogamy, the greater evil being to cause pain and ruin to ladies who may be in themselves innocent, since marriages are arranged by the elders of the family.

On the other hand, if any one of your wives decides to leave you, do not resist but welcome it. In so advising, we are pursuing another principle enunciated at I Corinthians 7:11. If the non-Christian leaves the Christian partner, the marriage is regarded as having been nullified (cf. I Cor. 7:15, 16). But do not force divorce yourself. We also welcome into the church your wives and children, if they themselves wish to be members of the church. After that we shall treat them as regular members of the church with full rights and privileges. They can receive the sacrament of the Eucharist. We shall finally require the polygynist and all his wives to give an undertaking to let their matrimonial compound be informed by the Christian ethic. In short, the church should proclaim "plenary indulgence" on polygynists who seek membership in the church.

It is gratifying to note that already some of the churches of Africa are acting along the lines suggested above, e.g., the Presbyterian Church of Ghana. Others are very selective and tend to apply this approach only in the case of chiefs who are obliged by tradition to have stool wives. We are humbly pleading for it to be the norm with such cases.

The other question—what should the church do with a member of the church who decides to contract a polygamous marriage?—is a more difficult issue, which we approach with great trepidation. Here we acknowledge that such a second marriage would constitute a willful violation of the law of the church and in full knowledge.[22] That calls for disciplinary action. What we are unsure of is the nature of the punishment. One is not happy with excommunication as the disciplinary measure, because marital and sexual errors are no worse than other errors, like a politician who squanders state funds.[23] Since hardly ever is the latter excommunicated, we do not see why a man who has been honest with his situation and circumstances should be penalized with excommunication. The usual penalty is debarring from the Lord's Supper. One can approve of that penalty as long as it is for a specific period of time and not forever. For if the Lord's Supper is a sacrament, as the Anglicans believe, and therefore a source of grace, then one cannot be happy with permanent exclusion from the Lord's Supper, because that would amount to denying the offender a source of grace which he certainly needs to mend his ways. In any case, the Eucharist is supposed to express also the fellowship of the community of believers (cf. I Corinthians 11). Therefore, to keep someone out of the Eucharist is in effect to declare him outside the fellowship. If so, then the church had better honestly declare such a one a non-Christian.

Here too—i.e., with regard to the Eucharist penalty—we wish to plead that this departure from the norm of monogamy is no worse than other deviations from the Christian norms. So in the interests of justice and equity, all offenders should be treated alike. Further, whatever decision is taken should be based on the full knowledge of the circumstances leading to his opting for polygamy. In other words, decision-makers should be on their guard against legalism. Certainly for a Christian to become a polygamist is a departure from a church norm which calls for disciplinary action. But the discipline should go with mercy and sympathy. Nevertheless, one would still advise against a polygamist holding a position or office within the church organization. For since leadership is *inter alia* an advertisement of what the society stands for, positions should be given to those who would create the least offense or bad image for the church.

Before we turn to the norms within marriage, let us address ourselves to the question of marriages between Christians and non-Christians. On this issue our situation in Africa is not unlike the situation of the church of Corinth (I Cor. 7:12 ff). It appears the issue in I Corinthians is a couple already married and one of them turning to Christianity. In the view of Paul the change of religion by one party need not affect the marriage. The implication is that the two were in a valid married state. Further, for the sake of the Christian party the non-Christian party is by God's grace sanctified. However, if the change of religion so bothers the non-Christian party as to make him desire to break up the marriage, the Christian party can accept the separation. But such a separation should not be at the instance of the Christian party. This has been known as the "Pauline exception" (I Cor. 7:15-16). It is a matter of the clash of two different systems and principles, and "every one [should] lead the life which the Lord has assigned to him, and in which God has called him" (I Cor. 7:17 RSV).

The question of whether one who is already a Christian may marry a non-Christian is not dealt with in the New Testament. But for ourselves there is nothing to rule such a union out of court. Only the Christian should ensure that it will not affect his Christian profession. In other words, they should count the cost before they enter the union.

Now, we return to the matter of the relationships within marriage. As we mentioned above, the matrimonial home and life should be informed by the Christian ethic of love, or selfless and self-sacrificing devotion to the other partner. Here it is important to look at Ephesians 5:21 ff.

Marriage is not just a partnership in the Christian view. Nor is it just profane; but it shares in a new creation. It is patterned on the prototype of the relationship between Christ and his church. It is meant to reflect the loving mutuality and fellowship which exists between Christ and the church. That mutuality is best expressed by the selfless and self-sacrificing devotion of Christ to his church and to men. To this extent marriage is a *sacramentum* (cf. Greek, *musterion*—Eph. 5:32).

The Christ-church paradigm and the biblical understanding of order in creation determine the relationships within marriage. There is some hierarchy in the home; the husband is the head, then the wife and then children. And of course, Christ is the head of the household (I Cor. 11:3; Eph. 5:23-24; Col. 3:18-19; Tit. 2:5; and I Pet. 3:1 ff). But such a hierarchy is designed to produce order and harmony and not to enable the men to tyrannize their wives. The men are in turn asked to practice selfless and self-sacrificing devotion to their wives: "Love your wife as your own body." In other words, husbands should treat their wives as they would like their wives to treat them. That excludes bossiness, tyranny, and disregard of the dignity and feelings of the other party. Similarly, the children should be submissive to their parents. But that in no way permits the parents to provoke their children (Col. 3:21; Eph. 6:4), i.e., to tyrannize over them and so forth. Each stage of the hierarchy carries with it obligations and responsibilities, and all those out of love.

It may well be that on the subject of the relationships within the family, African traditional society has a lot to learn from Christianity. For it tends to encourage the husband to be a boss. It still has to learn that primacy of place is not the same thing as bossiness. Furthermore, in a matrilineal society a man should be encouraged to see his obligations to his own progeny rather than put his nephews first.

Traditionally, the institutional aspects of life, e.g., law, tradition, religion, and social customs, controlled society. Traditional rural life was much more cohesive than modern urban life.[24] Urban life offers crowded living conditions, freedom from social control, anonymity of the individual, and more opportunities for recreational activities, which separate rather than unite the family. The combined assualt of Western culture, Christianity, and other influences is leading to, perhaps accelerating, the break-up of African traditional society. There is, therefore, need for education on the subject of the family and marriage. Perhaps the church's greatest task now is not so much to pontificate but to begin to educate society on marriage with a sensitivity to the traditional values. Areas of education should include an analysis of the pressures toward marriage, wrong mate selection, interference of relatives in marriage, rigid views on a man's place and role in life, woman's over-anxiety to be recognized as the head of the house, and so on. This task of education should be directed at all sectors of the community, not only at aspiring couples. This task is also the task of parents. Part of the problem in Africa at the moment is that often parents are absolutely helpless at assisting their children in the area of marriage. That has been worse confounded by the rebelliousness and rush of youth in our day. It is the task of parents from fairly early on—we suggest about the time of puberty—to instruct the children in responsible parenthood and sex. And in the process of education, Christian thinkers must disentangle the authentic Christian message from the European cultural ethos with which the Christian message came to Africa.

VIII

The Ethics of Power

The question of power is of moment at this time when liberation theology is being proclaimed. For some of the liberation theology reads very much like a reversal of positions, this time with the oppressed in the saddle and seat of power treating their former oppressors to a dose of their own medicine. That state of affairs will be as immoral as the present racism involving the discrimination against the blacks. Besides, there is ample evidence from the history of a number of Third World countries that the very persons who lead their compatriots from oppression by foreigners to political freedom, soon become the oppressors of their own people.

Again, this failing is not the preserve of politicians alone. Churchman have been guilty of the same. Clergymen, for example, have sometimes behaved like tin gods, God's private secretaries, tyrannizing over their fellowmen. This is in part the story of the events leading up to the Protestant Reformation of the sixteenth century. Tyranny coming from a religious people cannot be sanctified or sanctioned; it is as immoral as when it comes from an atheist or agnostic or a politician.

Thus, now that Africans have gained power in church as in state, in commerce as in industry, it is time to take a look at the issue of power in our societies. Conscious of the diverse manifestations of

power—political, economic, religious/ecclesiastical, and so on—
one is hesitant to treat them all together. But one would still venture
to highlight points that will be common to all of them and just hope
that readers will be encouraged to read further on specific issues
elsewhere.

The middle sixties to the early seventies of this twentieth century
have seen *coup d'état* after *coup d'état* in Africa. For many observers
these *coups d'état* have been evidence of the incompetence and
inability of *homo Africanus* to wield political power, especially
political power in modern statecraft, properly. To my mind this
analysis is superficial and does not take seriously the immediate
historical circumstances leading to the overthrow of the governments. In reaction to the superficial analysis mentioned above,
Africans have often charged that the *coups d'état* are the result of the
interference of colonialists and neo-colonialists in the political
affairs of African states, as though the foreign powers were trying to
regain their former positions. After the revelations made at the
Rockefeller Commission in 1975 that the Central Intelligence
Agency of the United States was involved in political upheavals in
Latin America, it will be difficult and perhaps futile to try to deny the
possibility.

However, even when allowance has been made for external
interference, there still remains the issue of the historical
circumstances leading to the *coup d'état*. For almost invariably a
coup d'état has occurred when a nationalist leader has begun to
tyrannize his kith and kin. Thus the *coup d'état* of February 24,
1966, which toppled the government of Mr. Kwame Nkrumah, the
prince of African nationalism and *Conditor Ghaniensis Civitatis*,
was also occasioned by Mr. Nkrumah's tyranny of Ghanaians
marked by many detentions without trial and illegal deportations of
both persons claiming to be nationals and aliens for unproved
allegations.[1] Similarly, the *coup d'état* which toppled Mr.
Tombolbaye of Chad in 1975 was also the result of Mr.
Tombolbaye's tyranny, persecution, and execution of his nationals
in the name of Tchaditude, which so much as compelled nationals
to have facial marks. It can be affirmed that whatever else may be
involved in these *coups d'état*, they were also a reaction to the abuse
and misuse of power by a nationalist leader. In other words, the issue
is not just a matter of politics; it is as well a moral issue. As the Akan
say, "Wo de wom, meremfa memma wo" na ɛmaa ɔdecamfo dii

ewu—"I have a share in it, but I will not give it to you": this made the proud man commit murder. Men always react violently to extortion and fraud. Further, the *coups d'état* can be viewed positively as the quest for viable forms of government at a time when Africans have outgrown their political systems both before and during colonialism.

Again, since Adam left paradise, the history of mankind has been to a large extent one of violence, collective and individual, urban and rural guerrilla warfare, political assassinations, kidnapings, hijackings, and various other acts of terror. History has been full of brutalities. But in this twentieth century, violence has paraded brazenly, declaring itself to be the benevolent tool of history's laws; and modern technology provides unprecedented means for turning man into putty in the hands of fellow human beings and countrymen.

The common theme in all the diverse manifestations of violence is that they derive from the struggle of egotistical and group interests, the struggle for limitless power, the suppression of intellectual freedom and the propagation of mass myths often narrow-minded and grossly oversimplified.

The manifestations of violence and the *coups d'état* may be viewed as part of the struggle to have power properly expressed in an ever-changing society. Since one knows not whither he goes unless he knows whence he came, it is important to start the study of power with how the traditional society, such as the Akan of Ghana, perceived power before we turn to the biblical tradition.

Traditional Akan society was based on kinship, each family with its own head, who is a councillor. The society is hierarchized. According to a maxim, *obi da obi akyir*—one man lies or stands behind another. That saying affirms the hierarchy in society. And so the young stand under the elders, the elders under the family head, the family head under the head of the clan, the clan head under the chief, the chief under the ancestors, and the ancestors under God. But why is there this hierarchy?

Hierarchy is a matter of natural order. Thus, according to the Akan, *pata ase wɔ hen*—there is a chief even under a shed which is inferior to a home or a state. It is thus natural to have a hierarchy in any group of persons. Second, the hierarchy is necessary to ensure order. Thus they say that *nhyehyɛe pa nti mpanyin wɔ baabiara*—it is in the interests of good order and arrangement that there be leaders everywhere. Further, they say that *sakasakayɛ nyɛ nti na nsiesiei pa* wɔ hɔ—because disorder is not good, there is need for good organization. Thus, however small a group of people, there is an elder among them to ensure orderliness and peace of society. Third, in traditional society and to a very large extent even today, there is great respect for age: *Nea adi kan o, nea ɛreba o, nea akyɛ ne panyin*—age is more venerable than rank or youthfulness. The aged should command the respect of the young because the former are said to be nearer the ancestors by virtue of age and experience, and therefore are better able to understand the mysteries of life. Indeed, *panyin ano sen suman*—the words of an old man or elder are more than the words of the minor deities because he speaks from experience and wisdom. Or again, the Akan say *onipa a wanyin sen eduefo*—the experienced old man knows better than the magician.

The chief is the next higher rank to the elder *(panyin)*. "The chief who rules the tribe is chosen from a particular lineage by the heads of the other lineages. Kin-right and popular selection are thus combined in the choice of a ruler."[2] Further, he holds his position by virtue of being the link between the living and the dead, as is well demonstrated by his sacral role at festivals and other state rites. A society has to be arranged in some sort of hierarchy in order to exist peacefully. And such a hierarchy, in part at any rate, reflects the society's outlook on life. The highest authority goes to those with the skills the society prizes most highly. The society then endows such persons with symbols to underline their authority, e.g., the stool or the state sword of the Akans. Such authority springs from our inward, unquestioning authority of the hierarchy of the surrounding society as well as from our assumption that a high position in it really matters.

The chief is the zenith of power. Undiscerning scholars have claimed that the drift to autocracy, authoritarianism, and dictatorship in Africa has been the result of the conception of chieftaincy which allegedly made for dictatorship. It is true that there are elements which might suggest absolute power of the chief. For example, the chief at his installation is given a sword representing he power of life and death which the chief wields over his subjects. Again, two proverbs are suggestive of the dreaded power of the chief. First, *ɔhen nya wu a, na edɛ* "*ɔnye me ka*"—it is only when the chief is dead that a subject can say "he likes me." In other words, his rule is so tyrannical that one can only breathe freely when he is dead. Second, *ɔhen bi n'aber do wohum, na obi n'aber do wɔyer*—in one king's reign the citizens are treated with violence and roughly; but in another's reign the citizens are stretched. In other words, with a new king there is a new law. And a chief, while on the throne, makes what changes he thinks fit.[3]

However, these suggestions of dictatorial powers are more apparent than real[4] because there are inbuilt checks, which we will proceed to outline. The chief did not wield absolute power. By virture of the fact that "kin-right and popular selections are . . . combined in the choice of a ruler,"[5] the chief is responsible to the people through the heads of the lineages. There are several illustrations of the point.

(a) At the chief's enstoolment he swears an oath that whenever the people call him, he will respond. If he fails, he is liable to impeachment. (b) Several proverbs inculcate this. *Edɔm anaa nkoa dodow na ɛkyerɛ ɔhene tumi*—the king's power and greatness depend on the number of his subjects who so recognize his position. If they withhold their support, he cannot be chief. They also say *ɔhene ho bɛyɛ fɛw o, no ho bɛyɛ hu o, ofi n'ahenkwaafo*—the chief's dignity and authority are the sole concern of his retinue; they make or unmake him. Further, the Akan say *ɔhene bedi wo kasa a efi amanfo*—when a chief is going to counsel you to do something, he does so by the authority of the people. And for that reason he is not left to rule alone; he is given some councillors to think and plan with him. *ɔhen nya ahotsenafo pa a, nna n'amambu yɛ yie*—if a chief gets good councillors, his rule is good. Even if the chief stands first in society, he is expected to rule and go on the advice of the state elders, who are supposed to be in touch with the people outside the palace.

Since his power is from the people, the chief is obliged to listen to his people: *ɔhene aso tse dɛ sɔne; no mu akwan bɔbor apem*—the ears of a chief are like a strainer; there are more than a thousand ways to them. He has aids who help him to strain out the truth from the numerous stories he hears from his subjects. He listens to everything but does not act on gossip or rumors. He does not act on information indirectly received. The Akan again say *ɔhen aso tse dɛ son aso*—the chief's ears are as the ears of the elephant—he hears everything that goes on in his state. The chief who does not heed the advice and cries of his courtiers and people is often destooled; dictatorship is answered with destoolment.

Second, the chief's power is held under God and the ancestors, the twin pillars of Akan religion.[6] Thus when a chief begins a ritual dance, he first points his sword, a symbol of his office, to the skies in acknowledgment of the act that his power derives ultimately from God. Or again, some dance motions dramatized the phrase *Gye Nyame*—except God. In other words, although the chief's power is supreme, it is held under God and on trust from God, and is, therefore, to be wielded in accordance with the will of God.

Third, the office of a ruler is seen in terms of the good of the subjects. The power going with the office is not meant to be used for the chief's personal aggrandizement but is intended to promote the happiness of the society. They say *nea ɔde ne man nsɛ e no*—the head of the state does not ruin it. In other words, it is the duty of the head to seek the welfare of the state. The position is to be used for administrative and judicial purposes. The chief ensures law and order, the defenses of the tribe from outside attacks as well as settling intra-tribal problems. Thus the Akan say *akasakasa ba na ɔpanyin ka bi a, edwo, asom-dwoe ba*—when an elder arbitrates in a dispute, there is peace.

Fourth, even if the chief has primacy of place, he has some obligations. According to the Akan *ɔdehye anko a, akoa guan*—if the chief does not fight, the slave runs away. In other words, if the leaders of the people do not set a good example, the common people shirk their responsibility. Or again, *ɔdekuro ba pɛ n'ahohra a, onya*—if the son of a chief wants abuse, he gets it. In other words, however elevated a person may be in society, he maintains his dignity only by self-respect. And indeed, the people are obliged to react in no uncertain terms to the foolish acts of a leader. For they too are exhorted thus: *eyɛ foofoo a wɔdze wo sekan gua nankā*—if you remain quiet, others will use your knife to dress a snake. In other words, subjects forfeit their rights if they do not defend them.

Thus in Akan society the chief held primacy of place in society. He commanded the respect and obedience of those over whom he wielded power: *ade a ɔhene pɛ ma no*—the will of the chief must be done by his subjects. But that is not to be equated with absolute power and dictatorship. Power is to be used to the benefit of society. With power goes responsibility to and for the people over whom it is exercised.

Of course, today the society has become more complex than before. There are new elements, such as the meritocracy—the experts in medicine, the "bookmen," and others who by their education stand out in society. One believes the role of the meritocracy is no different from the traditional role of the elders. For they were recruited from the meritocracy of the time—the warriors, medicinemen, and so on.

One last comment: power is a delicate thing which has to be handled with great care: *tum te sɛ kosua*—power is like an egg. If it is not handled with great care, it destroys both the wielder and those over whom it is wielded. Further, its effect outlives the users: *Ememen asekan dze dzi hen a, nyia obedzi w'adze no renye a, ɔfona*— if a chief is accustomed to swallowing knives, his successor experiences much difficulty when he relieves himself. In other words, a bad chief or the misuse of power creates problems for his successors.

This is a very brief introduction to the conception of power in Akan society. We wish not to suggest that there is some similarity between the Christian and traditional viewpoints with regard to power. In the biblical tradition, creation is hierarchized. Thus for example, in Psalm 8, man stands above creation. In the words of the psalmist:

> What is man that thou art mindful of him
>   and the son of man that thou dost care for him?
> Yet thou hast made him little less than God,
>   and dost crown him with glory and honor.
> Thou hast given him dominion over the works of thy hands;
>   thou hast put all things under his feet.
>   (Ps. 8:4-6 RSV; cf. Gen. 1:26 ff).

Man wields power and authority over the lower creation, and that under God. There is a hierarchy in the created order. Man's role is that of a planter in God's garden and world, one who ensures order and beauty and harmony in creation.

Similarly and more explicitly, as Paul puts it in his letter to the Corinthian church, "The head of every man is Christ, the head of a woman is her husband, and the head of Christ is God" (I Cor. 11:3 RSV). There is a hierarchy in the world of men: with God standing at the top, then Christ, man, woman, and lower creation.

However, the Bible, like traditional Akan society, thinks of the hierarchy not only in terms of positions of authority but also in terms of the roles and functions (already defined by God) to be exercised under God. Thus not only are wives to be submissive to their husbands, but also husbands are obliged to exercise selfless and self-sacrificing devotion to their wives. Indeed, husbands are forbidden to tyrannize over their wives: "do not be harsh with them" (Col. 3:18-19). Again, children are called upon to accept the authority of their parents, while at the same time the fathers are warned against provoking the children (Col. 3:20-21). The Akan's version of it is *aburow dua ne ho a, ɔtotɔ*—if maize plants itself, it drops at random. In other words, if a child does not pay heed to the advice and authority of his elders, he gets into trouble. Similarly, slaves are called upon to accept the authority of the masters, while the masters themselves are also asked to remember that they too are slaves of the Lord Christ and God (Col. 4:1). The implication is that masters can expect from God the treatment they mete out to their slaves.

From the above, we may deduce that the power wielded by persons in the various stations of life and human existence is not absolute. In fact they are accountable to God. Hence the warning "the wrongdoer [ruler or ruled] will be paid back for the wrong he has done, and there is no partiality" (Col. 3:25 RSV). In talking about power and authority, there is also some such thing as accountability, which is ultimately to God. Religious people who wield power, ostensibly unlimited, must feel themselves responsible before God and their own consciences. Other types of power are dangerous precisely because there are no higher values to check them.

The point of having a hierarchy is to have some order in society. Too many independent commanders will make for chaos. But in the biblical view, some sort of order is better than chaos and anarchy. Further, "God is not a God of confusion but of peace" (I Cor. 14:33 RSV). The creation stories of the book of Genesis tell the story of how God created order out of chaos and void. So when we speak of the hierarchy of the world and the power that goes with every station of life, our concern should be with the use of that power for creating order in society. We hasten to qualify the word "order"; we mean genuine order and not the semblance of order. This point is necessary because, in quite a few countries, when governments have tyrannized nationals, they have said it was in the interests of peace and order. And yet, upon examination, those actions of the government have been acts of terrorism. So it is necessary to emphasize genuine order. Whoever holds a position in the society does so in order to promote order, which in concrete terms covers such things as justice, i.e., the art of giving every man his due; peace;

the harmony and well-being of society; and freedom, which is not license but compatible with the freedom of others in the society, who also have dignity because they too bear the *imago Dei*.

At this point we must address ourselves to Romans 13. There Paul counsels submission to the state because "there is no authority except from God, and those that exist have been instituted by God" (Rom. 13:1 RSV) Akan man has a similar idea: *Nyina a obotum man hwɛ no, Nyankopɔn bɔ no safohen ma ɔdze kora dɔm*—it is God who enstools the talented leader as chief and commits the townsfolk to his care. This can be problematic. Is he saying that the dictatorial and oppressive governments such as we saw under Hitler of Germany, Nkrumah of Ghana, Tombalbaye of Chad, or the racist governments are also ordained by God? For to answer the question in the affirmative would be incompatible with the holiness, love, and the justice of God. Paul's statement was made with an eye on what is perceived to be the proper function of the state, which is clearly stated in the passage: the ruler "does not bear the sword in vain" (Rom. 13:4). The sword is, of course, the *jus gladii*, symbolizing blind justice which knows neither high nor low, rich nor poor, Caucasian nor Negroid. The "rulers are not a terror to good conduct, but to bad" (Rom. 13:3 RSV). And the definition of good conduct relates to both the will of God expressed in the society and the guidance of the Holy Spirit. The ruler "is the servant of God to execute his wrath on the wrongdoer" (Rom. 13:4 RSV). In short, the government should wield its power under God to achieve *pax et securitas*—peace and security of the entire community and the community of men everywhere.[7] One recalls Augustine's lines: "What is the state without justice? A band of robbers."

The implications of all this for the subject at hand are far-reaching. First, there is need for a hierarchy in society, with which goes some power. Hierarchy and power in themselves are not bad; they are neutral. Second, the crucial test of the power is that it should be used to promote order, peace, and security, to realize the claim that God is the God of order and not of confusion. As Dostoevsky put it in his *Diary of a Writer*, "An ethical idea has always preceded the birth of a nation." Third, power is to be perceived not only in terms of the position in the hierarchy but also in terms of its functions, roles, and objectives set by God. Power is limited and ephemeral because of this ultimate dependence on God (Luke 13:31-35). Fourth, since the power is held under God and should, therefore, be theocentric, there is excluded the naked use of power because that is egocentric. This last point needs illustrating.

Let us illustrate with Luke 9:51-56: James and John, the Bonanerges or sons of Thunder, were so incensed at the refusal of the Samaritans to welcome Jesus as to ask Jesus to call down fire to destroy them. Of course, human motives are often mixed: they may have called for fire also because of the old bitter strife between the Jews and the Samaritans (John 4:9).[8] Jesus' reaction is most instructive: he rebuked James and John. Jesus refused to use his power to crush those who rejected him and thereby kept themselves out of the kingdom of God which was, so to speak, knocking at their door in the person of Jesus of Nazareth. Even faith in God or in Christ cannot and should not be extorted or compelled. Naked use of power is ruled out whether in matters political or religious or economic. Jesus rejected the call of the Boanerges because that would have been the naked use of power, and that in its turn would be immoral because it would be egocentric rather than theocentric. This story should make the church bow her head in shame because down the centuries Christian people and institutions have persecuted unbelievers and heretics in the name of Christ. Thomas Aquinas represents a rather violent misuse of the church's power:

> From the point of heretics themselves there is their sin, by which they have deserved not only to be separated from the Church, but to be eliminated from the world by death. For it is far graver matter to corrupt the faith which is the life of the soul than to falsify money which sustains temporal life. So if it be just that forgers and other malefactors are put to death without mercy by the secular authority, with how much greater reason may heretics not only be excommunicated, but also put to death, when once [they] are convicted of heresy?[9]

Whether the church is in the minority or in the majority, force to induce faith is wrong. Equally wrong is the naked use of political power, and, for that matter, any form of power.

Again, there is ruled out power that is exploited and exploits. In his temptations, Jesus was put to the test to use the power accruing from being Son of God to get a following. He was tempted to be an economic Messiah to work an economic miracle in order to get Jewish following. He was also tempted to appear miraculously at the roof of the temple of Jerusalem in order to convince the people that he was the Messiah and Son of God. He was tempted to join forces with Satan, the prince of this world, in order to get a following. And Jesus rejected all these temptations to exploit his powers as the Son of God in order to entice the Jews to follow him. The proper goal for the use of power is that it serves God's purposes. Even that does not allow the naked use of power because that is the exploitation of power, which is egocentric in the first instance and not theocentric as it should be.

Furthermore, seeking power just for the sake of the power is ruled out because that too is egocentric. For example, the sons of Zebedee were given a rebuke for asking to be given the chief seats in the kingdom (Mark 9:34 f; 10:35-45). For power is for the service of man and God. There is a paradox about power and authority. Power viewed from the biblical standpoint involves both legal authority and humility. Thus "whoever would be great among you must be your servant, and whoever would be first among you must be slave of all" (Mark 10:43-44 RSV; Matt. 20:26-27). The paradox is that the one who has authority and power should behave as though he had no legal rights, indeed like a slave. He puts his own dignity and legal rights second to the well-being of those whom he rules. That power is to serve others in selfless and self-sacrificing service and devotion and through that, to help build the City of God.

In the Christian tradition one of the best examples of the understanding of power is found in the story of Jesus on the cross. When the passersby jeered at Jesus saying "Aha! You who would destroy the temple and build it in three days, save yourself, and come down from the cross!" (Mark 15:30), Jesus did nothing. Whether he ever actually threatened to destroy the temple or not is not our concern here. But to destroy the temple, which took over forty years to build, and to rebuild it in three days, would have been a remarkable and eloquent deed of power. That would have convinced everybody beyond doubt that he was a man of power. Of course, he had already shown power through the miracles he performed. And to have come down from the cross after all they had done to him would have been the miracle par excellence to dispel all unbelief, disbelief, and doubts about Jesus' power. In essence, that temptation was no different from the temptation to appear miraculously at the roof of the temple without any harm to himself. Yet that path would have been the naked display of power, emphasizing his own powers rather than pursuing the will of God.

It must have been a regular temptation all through Jesus' ministry to show power. Apart from the examples mentioned above, there is also Matthew 26:53. At the arrest, Jesus was tempted to show power: "Do you think that I cannot appeal to my Father, and he will at once send me more than twelve legions of angels?" (RSV). Presumably, the angels could fight for him and free him and possibly utterly destroy his enemies. But that would have been to put himself first and before God. And so Jesus adds to the question quoted above, "But how then should the scriptures be fulfilled, that it must be so?" (Matt. 26:54 RSV). The primary and constant concern is that God's will may be done. It may be our task as Christians, individually and severally, to encourage power-holders to put the will of God first, seeking that will in the light of all the available material.

Again, power should go with humility (Matt. 18:4; 23:12; Luke 14:11; 18:14).[10] Humility remains a Christian calling and norm (Phil. 2:5-8). Humility rules out the notion of infallibility, i.e., the idea that when a man of power and authority has spoken, then the only truth, the last word, has been spoken and cannot be questioned or criticized. Further, humility involves a sense in the man of power of his own inadequacies and failures. To put it another way, the man of power who is humble will be conscious that as long as he remains a mortal, he is as sinful and capable of mistakes as any other man. Third, the humble man is conscious of his limitations and submits to the guiding hand of God. Finally, as a Christian the humble man sets before his eyes the example of Christ, who did not insist too much on his status, who "when he was reviled, . . . did not revile in return; when he suffered, he did not threaten; but he trusted to him who judges justly" (I Pet. 2:23 RSV).

And so, our Christian conception of power is one of paradox: it is authority wielded in humility and sensitivity to others, the subjects included, and the one in power not insisting too much on his legal rights.

We now turn to the point made earlier about power being for service. The power of Jesus was used in response to the genuine needs of other people. It operated out of love and mercy. Thus the story of the feeding of the five thousand emphasizes that that act of power was out of compassion (Mark 6:34). It was not a matter of putting beneficiaries in his debt. It was a matter of the spontaneous (not calculated) response to the genuine needs of man. So at the end of the day the man of power can only say, "We are unworthy servants; we have only done what was our duty" (Luke 17:10 RSV).

This chapter so far, on the face of it, has been theoretical. This is deliberate. For the question of power affects all areas of life. There is political power; there is economic power; there is ecclesiastical power; there is the power of the press; there is parental power. These are only a few example of the diverse manifestations of the problem of power. We believe that what has been said in this chapter forms the basic principles for dealing with any of these manifestations of the problem of power. Again, the problem faces all nations. So we desired not to be parochial or too particular. And whether in Africa or America, in Europe or Asia or Australia, the principles outlined above hold good.

There is one aspect of the problem of power which we have skirted—namely, what response is to be made by the Christian subject to the person of authority who misuses his power, such as a dictator or an oppressive government. First, a Christian is obliged to pray for the ruler, more so if he is misusing his power: "I urge that supplications, prayers, intercessions, and thanksgiving be made for all men, for kings and all who are in high positions, that we may lead a quiet and peaceable life, godly and respectful in every way. This is good, and it is acceptable in the sight of God our Savior, who desires all men to be saved and to come to the knowledge of the truth" (I Tim. 2:1-4). To some, we believe, this would sound an unrealistic approach. For all the prayers of the churches did not stop Hitler misbehaving, not to mention the conflicting prayers stemming in part from self-interest in all men. The prayer should be that God may, if it be his will, change the tyrant to live as God intends him to live as the one who ensures peace and security for all men. Such a prayer is far from easy to pray for one who has buffetted you. So the obligation to pray for one's opponents, far from being the easiest option, is a difficult test of the Christian charity of an oppressed Christian. And such a prayer can be made only out of a deep love for another creature of God.

But prayers are not enough, nor are they alternatives to action. Not only did Jesus teach that the state commands the respect and cooperation of her citizens, but also that that submission to the state must be consonant with their obligations to God: "Render to Caesar the things that are Caesar's, and to God the things that are God's" (Mark 12:17 RSV). When the obligations to Caesar conflict with the obligations to God, then Christians must say, and act out, that "we must obey God rather than men" (Acts 5:29). A Christian is obliged to resist any form of the demonic powers; he is committed to actively working to put right injustices, whether to others or to oneself. A Christian is obliged to resist any system which demands total surrender of his soul—continuous and active participation in a general evil structure. There can be consent neither to the putrefaction of the soul nor to spiritual enslavement. This raises the rather big question of whether violence is admissible as a means of resisting tyranny.

We shall not attempt to give a cut- and-dried answer to this question. But we proffer the following guidelines. First, the position dictated by common sense, that a man should withdraw into his shell in order to survive, is a moral failure. For a Christian cannot be rightly neutral to moral issues that affect the dignity of man. Second, since the value of an action motivated by a sense of responsibility should not be determined by the chances of success, it is moral turpitude to do nothing with the excuse that it would be senseless to intervene against the obvious might of the dictator. The determining criterion for moral action is the obligation to be true to God's demands on man. Public opinion and chances of success do not come in. Third, God demands action, e.g., resistance which is a rebellion of conscience.

The nature of the action has to be arrived at after careful thought and prayer. Whether it be a violent overthrow or strikes or quiet resistance has to be arrived at in the light of the circumstances. We should guard against legalism and doctrinaire positions. In a case of the misuse of power, the principle for resisting should be "the greater good" or "the lesser of two evils." For I believe with Berdyaev that revolution can sometimes clear the air and reshuffle an existing balance of forces so as to open new channels for redemptive work. The assassination of a dictator can sometimes be more effective and actually reduce the sum total of violence better than a protracted conflict. [11] Further, whatever course one feels called to execute should aim at correcting injustice and not at retaliation. It should aim at restoring the dignity of both victim and aggressor.

We have stated both the biblical and Akan views with regard to power. We have noted similarities. The biblical ideas as outlined above are, we believe, absorbable by *homo Akanus*. So the specifically Akan statement of it would consist in reinforcing the main ideas with proverbs and maxims from Akan society. Further, the rites of installation to these offices of power should reflect these

ideas. And now let us attempt a brief statement of the biblical ideas of
power in an Akan society.

In God's world there is a natural hierarchy among people. For, as
the Akan say, *nsa yinara nsɛ*—not all fingers are the same; some are
shorter than others, and some are more powerful than others. We
cannot all be men of power; some must be ruled. Since it is God's
wish that some should be men of power, it may be said that some are
by divine ordination so created to be rulers. For, as the Akan put it,
*nyina a obotum man hwɛ no, Nyankopɔn bɔ no safohen ma ɔdze
kora dɔm*—it is God who enstools the talented leader as chief and
commits the townsfolk to his care. As such, the ruled should
recognize the chief's authority and power.

However, his position of power is for a specific purpose in God's
plan. A man of power is put there by God to use that power to work
for *ahotɔ* for his people. No one English word does justice to the
breadth of meaning of this Akan word. But it includes quiet,
quietness, peace, happiness, joy, comfort, comfortable feeling. For
as the Akan say, *nea ɔde ne man nsɛe no*—it is the chief's duty to seek
the welfare of the subjects. This means that God's purpose in setting
one up as a man of power is to promote justice, harmony of society,
genuine order, well-being, and freedom.

To achieve this, the man of power should be primarily concerned
not with his own dignity but with selfless and self-sacrificing
devotion to fellow men. As the Akan put it, *oku no ho ma ne
man*—he kills himself for his nation. He slaves away in the best
interests of his people so that they may have well-being. If the man of
power does that, he imitates the example of Christ, who, though
being in the form of God, humbled himself to die to make men
whole. This, to our mind, is the specifically Christian contribution
to the discussion of power. Further, he is entrusted with power so
that there may be proper form and order in society. For as the Akan
put it, *ano kɛse na ɛsɛ asɛnkɛsɛ*—it is the big mouth that should say
big things. In other words, if an important statement is to be made, it
has to be made by the man of power himself. That proverb is used to
inculcate the propriety of leaving important statements, announce-
ments, or requests to a person of importance. For too many bosses
bring about chaos. And the Christian affirms that his God is the God
not of confusion but of order. The role of the man of power is *inter
alia* to help forge such order in society.

Again, the position demands that the man of power should respect himself and comport himself with dignity. The Akan have two sayings which come in handy here. First, *opanyin ambɔ ne bra yie, mbofraba twetwe n'ase ahoma*—if an elder does not live a decent and respectable life, children will attempt to expose his nakedness to the public. This is used to inculcate the need for self-respect and dignity for the elder. Second, they say *ɔsɛdɛ panyin dzi no ho yi*—it behooves the elder to respect himself.

This last point implies accountability both to the spirit-world and to the subjects. On the one hand, the subjects recognize his authority by doing his will. But on the other hand, he is answerable to them for bad manners or for ignoring his part of the covenant relationship between them. That is why chiefs can be destooled. Again the subjects have a right, and are obliged, to react in no uncertain terms because, as we quoted above, *eyɛ foofoo a wɔdze wo sekan gua nankā*—if you do not defend your rights you forfeit them.

Finally, it is important that these ideas be dramatized through the rites relating to the installation to positions of power. That is a subject for a separate study.

Power can be good, but it has often plagued those who have wielded it. Hence the notorious acts of torture and brutality all over the world. Power all too often has become an instrument of terror. And so, we offer the prayer of the inscription standing in the city of Hiroshima to recall the unexampled terror and destruction by the powerful atom bomb dropped by the powerful United States, from an air force B29 called Enola Gay piloted by Colonel Tibbetts on August 6, 1945: For the victims of the misuse of power, and for the living, the prayer is:

> Rest in peace
> for the error
> shall never be repeated.

Select Bibliography

Agbeti, J. K. "Theological Education in Ghana 1943-63" in *Ghana Bulletin of Theology* 3(10): 23-34. 1971.

All African Council of Churches.*The Church in Changing Africa. Report of the All Africa Conference of Churches*. Ibadan. 1955.

Ayandele, E. A. *Holy Johnson*. London: F. Cass, 1970.

Baeta, C. G. *Prophetism in Ghana*. London: S.C.M., 1962.

———. *Christianity in Tropical Africa*: London: Oxford University Press, 1963.

Barrett, D. B. *Schism and Renewal in Africa*. Nairobi, 1968.

Becken, H. J., ed. *Relevant Theology for Africa*. Durban: Lutheran Publishing House, 1973.

Beetham, T. A. *Christianity and the New Africa*. London: Pall Mall Press, 1967.

Bosch, D. "Currents and Crosscurrents in South African Black Theology," in *Journal of Religion in Africa*, pp. 1-22. 1974.

Christian Council of Gold Coast.*Christianity and African Culture*. Accra: Christian Council of Gold Coast. 1955.

Desai, R., ed. *Christianity as Seen by the Africans*. Denver: A. Swallow, 1962.

Dickson, K. A. and Ellingworth P., ed. *Biblical Revelation and African Beliefs*. London: Lutterworth, 1969.

Dickson, K. A. *Aspects of Religion and Life in Africa*. Accra: Ghana Academy of Arts and Sciences, 1977.

Glasswell, M. E. "Sierra Leone Church: Local or Foreign," in *Liturgical Review* IV: 29-35. 1974.

————. and Fashole-Luke, E. W. *New Testament Christianity for Africa and the World.* 1974.

Glasswell, M. E. "Can there be an African or a Black Theology?" in *The Modern Churchman* XVIII (4): 164-172. 1975.

————. "The Quest of an African Christ," in *Ekklesiastikos Pharos* (Addis Ababa) LVIII, 114-18. 1976.

Goreham, J. "Towards an African Theology," in *Expository Times* LXXXVI (8): 233-36. 1975.

Hastings, A. *Christian Marriage in Africa.* London: S.P.C.K., 1973.

————. *African Christianity.* London: Chapman, 1976.

Hillman, E. *Polygamy Reconsidered.* Maryknoll: Orbis, 1975.

Idowu, E. Bolaji. *Towards an Indigenous Church.* London: Oxford University Press, 1965.

Ilogu, E. *Christianity and Ibo Culture.* Leiden: E. J. Brill, 1974.

Jacobs, D. R. *Christian Theology in Africa.* U.S.A.: Mount Joy, 1966.

Johnson, T. S. *The Story of a Mission.* London: S.P.C.K., 1953.

Kato, B. H. *African Cultural Revolution and the Christian Faith.* Jos, Nigeria: Challenge Publications, 1976.

————. *Black Theology and African Theology in Perception.* Publication of Evangelists of Africa and Madagascar, October, 1976, pp. 1-8.

————. *Theological Pitfalls in Africa.* Kisumu, Kenya: Evangel Publishing House, n.d.

Mbiti, J. S. *New Testament Eschatology in an African Background.* London: Oxford University Press, 1971.

————. "Some Current Concerns in African Theology," in *Expository Times* LXXXVII (6): 164-68. 1976.

————. *African and Asian Contributions to Contemporary Theology.* Celigny: W.C.C. Ecumenical Institute, 1977.

Mobley, H. W. *The Ghanaian's Image of the Missionary, An Analysis of the Published Critiques of Christian Missionaries by Ghanaians 1897-1965.* Leiden: E. J. Brill, 1970.

Moore, B., ed. *Black Theology: The South African Voice.* London: Hurst, 1973.

Mulago, V. *Un visage africaine du Christiansme* Paris: Presence Africaine, 1965.

Nyamiti, C. *African Theology.* Kampala: Gaba Pastoral Institute, 1974.

Pobee, J. S., *Religion in a Pluralistic Society.* Leiden: E. J. Brill, 1976.

Sawyerr, H. A. "Traditional Sacrificial Rituals and Christian Worship," in *Sierra Leone Bulletin of Religion* 2 (1): 18-27. 1960.

————. "A Sunday Graveside Libation in Freetown after a Bereavement," in *Sierra Leone Bulletin of Religion* 9 (2): 41-45. 1967.

————. *Creative Evangelism.* London: Lutterworth, 1968.

Shorter, A. *African Cultures and the Christian Church.* Dublin: G. Chapman, 1973.

Smith, Edwin. *African Beliefs and Christian Faith* London, 1943.

Sundkler, Bengt. *Bantu Prophets in South Africa.* London: Oxford University Press, 1961.

Taylor, J. V. *Primal Vision.* London: S.C.M., 1967.

Thomas, J. C. "What is African Theology?" in *Ghana Bulletin of Theology* 4 (4): 14-30. 1973.

Turner, V. W. *Schism and Continuity in an African Society*. Manchester, 1957.

Ukpabio, Esien. *Esere, As Seen Through African Eyes* Logos, 1916.

Williamson, S. G. *Akan Religion and the Christian Faith* Accra: Ghana Universities Press, 1965.

Notes

Chapter I

1. Speech at Conference of Independent African States, Accra, April 15, 1958, p. 13.
2. *Daily Graphic*, December 12, 1950.
3. Marcus Garvey, *The Philosophy and Opinions of Marcus Garvey*, Amy Jacques Garvey, ed. (New York: Atheneum, 1969), p. 44.
4. S. G. Williamson, *Akan Religion and the Christian Faith* (Accra: Ghana University Press, 1965), pp. 175-76.
5. The disappearance of indigenous peoples has been due to a number of factors: (a) their extermination by immigrant Europeans; (b) extermination by disease and alcoholism, some of which were brought by Europeans; (c) the destruction of their religious ideas and rituals, and of their way of life which gave meaning to their existence. The improvement of their living conditions through the organization of medical aid, new types of crops, farm animals, and the obstruction of tribal wars also had the effect of making the natives apathetic. They began to age prematurely, lose the will to live, and become less immune to diseases they previously naturally survived with ease. The result was the plummeting of the birth rate, and a dwindling population.
6. G. E. Ladd, *The New Testament and Criticism* (London: Hodder & Stoughton, 1967), p. 196.
7. E. Husserl, *Ideas* (London: Allen and Unwin, 1931).
8. P. Tillich, *Systematic Theology* (Chicago: University of Chicago Press, 1951), I, 118.

Chapter II

1. This universal claim has been called in question by A. R. Lovejoy, *The Great Chain of Being* (New York: Harper, 1960) pp. 99-143, esp. pp. 101-3. His argument is that "what is as poetically and religiously significant in the older

cosmography was, then, little touched by the Copernican theory" (p. 103). However, for this essay we shall take our stand with the traditional view.

2. R. Passmore and J. S. Robson, eds., *A Companion to Medical Studies* (Oxford: Blackwell Scientific Publications, 1968), 5:23.

3. A. Richardson, *University and Humanity* (London: S.C.M., 1964), p. 29.

4. K. A. Busia, *Africa in Search of Democracy* (London: Routledge & Kegan Paul, 1967), p. 1.

5. R. S. Rattray, *Ashanti* (London: Oxford University Press, 1923), Rattray, *Religion and Art in Ashanti* (Oxford University Press, 1927); K. A. Busia, "The Ashanti of the Gold Coast" in *African Worlds: Studies in the Cosmological Ideas and Social Values of African Peoples*, ed. D. Forde (Oxford University Press, 1954); S. G. Williams, *Akan Religion and the Christian Faith* (Accra: Ghana University Press, 1965).

6. Lactantius, *Epitome Divinarum Institutionum* 54, in *Patrologiae Latinae* 6:1061.

7. *"Theotokos"* is capable of two interpretations: (a) It could be understood of the God-Person, i.e., the component *"Theos"* (God) is a predicate. That is the sense in which Nestorius was prepared to allow its use and to treat as orthodox. (b) It could be used of the God-Nature, i.e., God is subject. That, to him, would be heresy. The problem, put in everyday language, is the difference between "who gave birth to God" and "the mother of God."

8. J. Macquarrie, *Principles of Christian Theology* (London: S.C.M., 1966), p. 1.

9. W. Pannenberg, *Revelation as History* (London: Macmillan, 1969). This represents our understanding of the subject.

10. Macquarrie, *Principles of Christian Theology*, p. 75.

11. K. Cragg, *The Call of the Minaret* (London: Oxford University Press, 1956), pp. 35 ff.

12. W. Robertson Smith, *Religion of the Semites* (London: Black, 1907), pp. 16-17; A. R. Radcliffe-Brown, *Structure and Function in Primitive Society* (London: Cohen & West, 1952).

13. E. Conze, *Buddhist Scriptures* (Harmondsworth: Penguin, 1959); *Wisdom Gone Beyond: An Anthology of Buddhist Texts* (Dawson, 1967); R. C. Zaehner, ed., *Bhagavad-Gita* (Oxford: Clarendon, 1969); Zaehner, ed., *Hindu Scriptures* (London: 1966).

14. M. Posnansky, "Archaeology, Ritual and Religion" in *The Historical Study of African Religion*, ed. T. O. Ranger and I. Kimambo (London: Heinemann, 1972), pp. 29-44.

15. For lengthy discussions of the word, see E. G. Parrinder, *African Traditional Religion* (London: Hutchinson's University Library, 1954), pp. 15 ff; Rattray, *Ashanti*, pp. 9 ff; Rattray, *Religion and Art*, pp. 24 f. E. Bolaji Idowu, *African Traditional Religion: A Definition* (London: S.C.M., 1973), pp. 108-36.

16. F. J. Leenhardt, *The Epistle to the Romans* (London: Lutterworth, 1961), p. 62.

17. It has sometimes been asserted that "emotion is completely Negro, as reason is Greek." We do not subscribe to this assertion.

18. My colleague, the Rev. Dr. J. C. Thomas, has rightly drawn my attention to the fact that a man's experience of the world can be distorted. For example, a juvenile delinquent who is so because of how his father treated him, will almost certainly find it difficult to appreciate any talk of the love of God. This warning is accepted. However, it only confirms us in our view that a man's experiences influence his theology. In the case under review, he will probably emphasize the wrath of God.

19. O. Mannoni, *Prospero and Caliban: The Psychology of colonization* (New York: Praeger, 1964); originally *Psychologie de la Colonisation* (Paris: Editions du Seuil, 1950). Sir Alan Burns, *Colour Prejudice* (London: Allen and Unwin,

1948). Mayotte Capecia, *Je suis Martiniquaise* (Paris: Corréa, 1948). Jean Veneuse, *Un homme pareil aux autres* (Paris: Editions Arc en Ciel, 1947). Aimé Cesaire, *Discours sur le colonialisme* (Paris: Présence Africaine, 1956).

20. J. H. Cone, *Black Theology and Black Power* (New York: The Seabury Press, 1969); C. Long, "The Black Reality: Toward a Theology of Freedom" in *Criterion*, Spring-Summer, 1964; J. Deotis Roberts, *Liberation and Reconciliation* (Philadelphia: Westminster Press, 1967).

21. Deotis Roberts, *Black Political Theology* (Philadelphia: Westminster Press, 1974), p. 80.

22. M. L. King, *Stride Toward Freedom* (New York: Harper, 1958).

23. J. A. Banks and J. D. Grambs, *Black Self-Concept* (New York: McGraw-Hill Paperbacks, 1972).

24. E. Lincoln, "The Black Church in America" in *Mission Trends*, ed. G. H. Anderson and T. F. Stransky, C.S.P. (New York, 1974), p. 82.

25. W. H. Grier and P. M. Cobbs, *The Jesus Bag* (New York: McGraw Hill, 1971), p. 180.

26. Cited in *Malcolm X: The Man and His Time*, ed. J. H. Clarke (New York: Collier, 1969), p. 159. In the same volume the Rev. Mr. Albert Cleage adopts the same militant stand. See his "Myths about Malcolm X," pp. 13-26, esp. pp. 22-23.

27. Harrison E. Salisbury, ed., *Sakharov Speaks* (New York: Vintage, 1974), p. 66.

28. *Ibid.*, p. 204-5.

29. Cited by Peter Berger in "Religion" in *Fortune*, Special Bicentennial Issue: The American System, April 1975, p. 134.

30. K. A. Busia, "The African World View" in *Christianity and African Culture* (Accra: Christian Council of Ghana, 1955), p. 1.

31. K. Cragg, *Christianity in World Perspectives* (London: Lutterworth, 1968), p. 74.

32. S. J. Semartha, "Dialogue as a Continuing Christian Concern" in *Mission Trends* 1, pp. 256-58; J. K. Matthews, *A Church Truly Catholic* (New York, 1969).

Chapter III

1. For a shorter statement, see J. S. Pobee, "Aspects of African Religion", in *Sociological Analysis*, Vol. 37, No. 1, pp. 1-18; J. S. Pobee and E. H. Mends, "Social Change and African Traditional Religions" in *Sociological Analysis*, Vol. 38, No. 1, pp. 1-12.

2. K. A. Busia, *The Position of the Chief in the Modern Political System of Ashanti: A Study of the Influence of Contemporary Social Changes on Ashanti Political Institutions* (London: Oxford University Press, 1951), p. 39.

3. *Som* means either to give respect or to serve or to worship. A child will *som* the father, i.e., serve the father, as well as *som* God, i.e., worship God. This is perhaps a reminder that the jump from veneration to worship is not too sharp.

    Some scholars suggest that *abosom* derives from a conversion of *som bo*, that which is precious to the owner, e.g., K.K.A. Ante, *Relationship between the Supreme Being and the Lesser Gods of the Akan*, M.A. Thesis, Department of the Study of Religions, University of Ghana (1978), pp. 36 ff.

4. Busa, in *African Worlds: Studies in the Cosmological Ideas and Social Values of African Peoples*, ed. D. Forde (London: Oxford University Press, 1954), pp. 199-200.

5. See my "Funerals in Ghana" in *Ghana Bulletin of Theology*, Vol. 4, No. 5, pp. 17-29.

Chapter IV

1. G. Every, *Misunderstandings Between East and West* (London: Lutterworth Press, 1965); Every, *The Byzantine Patriarchate* (London: S.P.C.K., 1962).

2. K. A. Busia, "Ancestor Worship, Libation, Stools, Festival" in *Christianity and African Culture*, ed. S. G. Williamson (Accra: Christian Council of Ghana, 1955), p. 18. W. Robertson Smith, *Religion of the Semites*, pp. 16-17. See also the functional theories of Fustel de Coulanges, Durkheim, Loisy.

3. Hinderer to Venn, Nov. 15, 1864: C.M.S. CA 2/049.

4. *A Hundred Years 1848-1948: The Story of the Presbyterian Training College, Akropong* (Akropong, 1948), p. 6. See also J. S. Pobee, "Church and State in the Gold Coast in the Vasco da Gama Era" in *Journal of Church and State* (Waco, Tex.: Baylor University Press, 1975), Vol. 17, No. 2, pp. 217-37.

5. J. W. C. Wand, *A History of the Early Church* (London: Methuen, 1937), p. 8.

6. Adaptation is the term used by Vatican II. Some scholars find *accommodation* unsatisfactory because it allegedly implies a looking down at African beliefs. I myself am not so persuaded. In any case, I believe a word is as good as we make it. But to avoid unnecessary argument I shall call it the positive approach. See G. Wainwright, "The Localization of Worship" in *Studia Liturgica*; 1971–72, pp. 26-41.

7. R. E. S. Tanner, *Transition in African Beliefs* (New York, 1967), p. 122.

8. Quoted by S. H. Rooy, *The Theology of Missions in the Puritan Tradition* (Grand Rapids: Eerdmans, 1965), pp. 30-31.

9. J. Hunt, "On the Negro's Place in Nature" in *Memoirs of the Anthropological Society of London. 1863–1864* (London), pp. 26-27, 51-52.

10. Aimé Cesaire, *Introduction to Victor Schoelcher Esclavage et colonisation* (Paris: Presses Universitaires de France, 1948), p. 7.

11. Cited by H. Debrunner, *A History of Christianity in Ghana* (Accra: Waterville Press, 1967), p. 145.

12. Correspondence from Chief Atcherey to Brandford-Griffith dated February 16, 1887, and Despatch No. 396 from White to Holland dated October 31, 1886; CO/96/184.

13. G. G. Findlay and W. W. Holdsworth, *The Wesleyan Methodist Missionary Society* (London: Epworth, 1922), IV, 175.

14. Nene Azu Mate Kole, "The Historical Background of Krobo Customs" in *Transactons of the Historical Society of Ghana*; Vol. I, Part IV (Achimota, 1955), p. 136.

15. *Native Customs Ordinance*, Vol. II, Cap. 112, Section 4. W. Schlatter, *Geshichte der Basler Mission 1815–1915* (Basel: Missionsbuchandlung, 1916), III, 152.

16. J. B. Danqyah, *Ancestors, Heroes and God. The Principles of Akan-Ashanti Ancestor-Worship and European Hero-Worship* (Kebi, Gold Coast, 1938). P. A. Sarpong, *Ghana in Retrospect: Some Aspects of Ghanaian Culture* (Accra: State Pubishing Co., 1974), p. 338. K. A. Opoku, "Aspects of Akan Worship" in the *Black Experience in Religion*, ed. C. E. Lincoln (Garden City, N.Y.: Doubleday Anchor Books, 1974), p. 293.

17. J. H. Nketia, *Drumming in Akan Communities* (London: Nelson, 1963); Nketia, *Music in African Cultures*, Legon: University of Ghana (1966); Nketia, *Folk Songs of Ghana* (University of Ghana, 1963).

18. K. A. Busia, *Report on a Social Survey of Sekondi-Takoradi* (London: Crown Agents for the Colonies, 1950); Busia, "Has the Christian Faith Been Adequately Represented?" in *I.R.M.*, 1961, pp. 86-89; Busia, *Address to the Closing Session of the Pan-Africano-Malagasy Laity Seminar*, August 18, 1971.

19. W. Knight, *Memoir of Henry Venn* (London, 1882), Appendix C, pp. 412-37. E. A. Ayandele, *The Missionary Impact on Modern Nigeria 1842-1914* (London: Longmans, 1966), pp. 180 ff.; *The Church and Native Customs* (Lagos: C.M.S. Press, 1914); Esién Ukpabio, *Esere, As Seen Through African Eyes* (Lagos, 1916).

20. S. G. Williamson, "The Lyrics in the Fanti Methodist Church" in *Africa*, April 1958, pp. 128 ff.

21. M. S. O'Rorke, *Life and Work in the Diocese of Accra During 1922* in *S.P.G. Report* (1922).

22. *Golden Shore*, April 1943, p. 137.

23. K. S. Latourette, *A History of Christian Mission in China* (New York, 1929), pp. 132-55; G. Dunne, *Generation of Giants* (London, 1962).

24. *Missale Romanum Auctoritate Pauli V Pont. M.* Sinice redditum A.P. Ludovic O. Buglio, Pekin in College ejus d. Soc. A.N. MDCLXX.

25. P. Freire, *Pedagogy of the Oppressed* (New York: Seabury Press, 1974), esp. chap. 2 and 3.

26. R. Peil, *A Handbook of the Liturgy* (London: Herder, 1960), pp. 35 ff.

27. J. H. Brauer, *Die Missions-Anstalten und Gesellschaften der evangelischen Kirche des Europäischen Vestlandes*, Part II (1851), pp. 660-61.

28. J. Héring, *The Epistle to the Hebrews* (London: Epworth, 1970), p. 36.

29. F. J. Leenhardt, *The Epistle to the Romans* (London: Lutterworth, 1961), p. 62.

30. *Ibid.*, p. 63.

31. F. F. Bruce, *The Epistle to the Hebrews* (Edinburgh: T. & T. Clark, 1942), p. 2. J. Héring, *Epistle to the Hebrews*; pp. 1-2.

32. Aratus, *Phaenomena* 5; Cleanthes, *Hymn to Zeus*, 5.

33. Leenhardt, *The Epistle to the Romans*, p. 82.

34. "Funeral Orations" by Saint Gregory Nazianzen and Saint Ambrose in *Fathers of the Church*, Vol. 22 (New York: Fathers of the Church, 1953), No. 6, p. 123.

35. H. Conzelmann, "The Address of Paul on the Areopagus" in *Studies in Luke-Acts*, ed. L. E. Keck and J. L. Martyn (Nashville: Abingdon, 1966), pp. 217-30. N. B. Stonehouse, *Paul Before the Areopagus* (London: Tyndale, 1957), pp. 1-40.

36. J. Mbiti has done great service to us by collecting the names of God outlining the attributes of God. See his *African Religions and Philosophy* (London: Doubleday, 1969). See also A. Shorter, *African Culture and the Christian Church* (New York: Orbis, 1974), p. 56.

Chapter V

1. My colleague Joshua Kudadjie has questioned whether Christology stands at the heart of the Christianity-African culture encounter. He suggests that such a conclusion is as seen by a European theologian or European-trained African. He further suggests that for the African there is no *one heart* but many points, all of them important, namely the presuppositions, particularly concerning men, e.g., the Fall, concept of salvation. Christology itself seems to be not the central problem, but only one of them; *homo Africanus* is not preoccupied with speculations of this kind, but with efficacy, the results of his religion for the worshiper. He concludes that if a Christology is worked out to the satisfaction of the African then Christianity might have full meaning for him.

This is a valid comment if we consider how most people actually operate when they address themselves to Christianity. However, Christian evangelism is a proclamation about Christ. As Paul puts it, "we preach Christ and him crucified." In any case, the concept of salvation, which is the other side of the coin of the Fall, makes sense only because of some affirmations made about Christ as the means of salvation from sin, legation, self-sufficiency, and the cosmic powers. Similarly without certain assertions about Jesus Christ it is meaningless to see Jesus as the turning point of history, and eschatology will be unpreachable or at least will lack a solid base. Therefore, we still maintain that Christology stands at the heart of the encounter between Christianity and African culture.

Again, one is unhappy with the assertion that African man is concerned with the efficacy of his religion. This, of course, rules out the height of Christian devotion, namely disinterested piety which can say at all times "Thy will be done." Efficacy is not the index of true religion. Rather, true piety is when one can say through thick and thin, with Polycarp of Smyrna, "Four score and ten years have I served him and he has done me no wrong. . . . Wherefore should I deny my king?" Polycarp's zeal was rooted in his Christology, his affirmation of Jesus as King. In any case, undue emphasis on efficacy soon leads to a barter with God, which authentic biblical faith denounces as being of the essence of sin.

In view of all these considerations one is unrepentant in asserting that Christology stands at the heart of any evangelism.

2. My colleague J. Christopher Thomas has expressed his dissatisfaction with my opposition between the Creed and the New Testament. According to him the problem is deeper than that: first, the New Testament is not a theologically or philosophically innocent document. It contains large lumps of Hebrew theology and Greek philosophy. If these are removed very little, if anything, is left. He is doubtful if we can get back to a simple gospel which is conceptually neutral. Second, he argues that the primary source for the first hundred to hundred and fifty years of the church's life was presumably not the New Testament as we know it, but rather the apostolic tradition. And so, he asks, does not the appeal to the New Testament alone make any new Christology evolved sectarian in favor of Protestantism? A further question he raises is that if we are remaking Christian doctrine from the start, do we not have to raise questions about the canon of the New Testament? That is, was the early church correct in selecting the books she did? If on the other hand, the decision about the canon of the New Testament is accepted, then why not other decisions made at the same time?

These comments are question marks against the basic assumptions of the study. Some of it we touched on in the Prolegomena. We recognize that these are questions which require volumes to do justice to them, not just passing references in a chapter of a book. Nevertheless, let us in a brief compass attempt to react to them.

First, I do not exactly make an opposition between the New Testament and the Creed. Rather we assert that the Creed itself must be checked against the biblical affirmations about Jesus Christ, the latter being the primary source of the church's faith, if for no other reason than that they are the earliest attempts at putting in written form the traditions that circulated orally for some time in the earliest congregations. This being my understanding of the situation with regard to sources, I do not accept the charge of being sectarian in favor of Protestantism. Indeed in chapter 1, I insist on the tradition of the early church. In any case, I suggest that both the New Testament and the Creed agree on the essentials of Christology, namely the humanity and divinity of Jesus Christ. So it is beside the point to raise questions of canon here.

Second, I am not claiming that we can get back to a simple gospel which is conceptually neutral. Surely, biblical criticism has long realized that the Gospels, for example, are portraits of Christ by men of faith for men of faith. But this makes it all the more remarkable that at the end of the day all the traditions come to agree on the twin pillars of the humanity and divinity of Jesus. And that is the firm rock which we are attempting to translate.

3. O. Cullmann, *Christology of the New Testament* (London: S.C.M., 1963).
4. L. A. Boadi, "The Language of the Proverb in Akan" in *African Folklore* ed. R. M. Dorson (Garden City, N.Y.: Doubleday, 1972), p. 183. Elizabeth Amoah, *Moral and Social Significance of Proverbs Among the Wassaws—An Akan People* (M.A. Thesis at the University of Ghana, 1974), esp. chapter 1 (pp. 1-63). J. B. Christensen, "The Role of Proverbs in Fante Culture," in *Africa*, Vol. 28 (London: Oxford University Press, 1958).
5. The form in which the miraculous birth of Jesus is couched is that of "a divine overcoming of a stumbling block and counteracting of misunderstanding and slander." (K. Stendahl, "Matthew" in new and rev. ed. of *Peake's Commentary* (Edinburgh, 1962), col. 647, p. 771.
6. R. Brown in *Theological Studies*, 26 (1965), pp. 545-73.
7. J. Héring, *The Epistle to the Hebrew* (London: Epworth, 1970), p. 36.
8. R. Brown, *The Gospel according to John I–XII* (Garden City, N.Y.: Doubleday, 1966), p. 345.
9. Akan society is by and large matrilineal. In other words, for purposes of inheritance a man belongs to his mother's family, even though he has obligations on his father's side. However, there are other African groups, like the Gās and Ewes of Ghana, who are patrilineal, i.e., for purposes of inheritance a man belongs to his father's family. It seems that, in the case of Jesus, the patrilineal system is more appropriate.
10. K. Antubam, *Ghana's Heritage of Culture* (Leipzig: Koehler, 1963), p. 65. The saying makes two affirmations: death as a characteristic of man and the indeterminacy of the coming of death. Our interest is in the former of the two points.
11. *Ibid.*, p. 66.
12. Joshua Kudadjie has raised a question of methodology with regard to expressing Jesus' humanity by way of pointing out similarities between Jewish view of humanity and the Akan. It seems to him that the approach should be: "What does the Akan understand the person of Jesus to be? He need not accept the conclusion of Greco-Hellenistic-European theologians that Jesus is human-divine, and then see whether the Akan also sees Jesus thus." He is "advocating for a radically different approach—as if the Akan were the first to work out a Christology. How would he do it, from his knowledge of Jesus in the Gospels?"

First, let us say we are unable to accept that Akan man has any choice about Jesus being human-divine. That is the nonnegotiable affirmation of the church, whether Judeo-Christian or Hellenistic Christian. Surely this was what the christological controversies of the first four centuries were about and the councils asserted. So that is a given affirmation of the church. One cannot repudiate it without coming close to heresy. Again, the suggestion that Akan man must behave as though he were the first is an impossibility. For as a matter of fact he cannot do otherwise. That suggestion is only raising the much more difficult problem of the facts about Jesus, whom Akan man did not see. That approach seems to us to be wild goose chasing. Third, we ourselves are persuaded of the similarities between Akan man's world view and the Semitic and biblical world view. At least the evidence adduced in this section is an argument in favor of that view, not to mention the works of Kwesi A. Dickson, J. B. Danquah, Modupe Oduyoye, even if we take some of the linguistic arguments *cum grano salis*.

In view of these arguments we feel it more fruitful to proceed by the similarities between Akan and Jewish views of humanity. That is to go from the known to the unknown.

13. See F. B. Welbourn, "Some Problems of African Christianity: Guilt and Shame" in *Christianity in Tropical Africa*; ed. C. G. Baeta (London: Oxford University Press, 1968), pp. 182-99.

14. See also Elizabeth Amoah, *Moral and Social Significance of Proverbs*, chapter 3, pp. 129-60. J. B. Danquah "Obligation in Akan Society" in *West African Affairs*, Vol. 8 (London: Bureau of Church Affairs, 1952).

15. A third way of refering to the sinlessness of Jesus and therefore his divinity would be through the numenal or ethical sense of his being pure, holy. One is not sure that these two words do justice to the biblical conception. It may be good to add words like *koronkoron* (sanctity) and *hotewee* (cleanliness). One is not sure how *mysterium tremendum* may be interpreted into Akan. In any case, one suspects all this is covered when we talk of the sinlessness of Jesus.

16. Williamson, *Akan Religion and the Christian Faith* (Accra: Ghana University Press, 1965), p. 92. Kudadjie has questioned our understanding of heavy *kra*. He comments, "One is said to have a heavy *kra* not because he performs some wonders, but because he is unconquerable by evil spirits, accidents etc." We are unhappy about contrasting the performance of wonders and unconquerableness by evil spirits. For in traditional society the latter is proved by the former, since all evil is attributed to personal forces of evil. Consequently, to cure amounts to sharing greater power than the evil spirits that caused the original havoc.

17. In Akan society *Nana* is used of the illustrious ancestor as well as of the Supreme Being, called *Nana Nyame*. That may indicate that the ancestors live in the court of God and exercise some authority under God.

18. Busia, *Africa in Search of Democracy* (London: Routledge & Kegan Paul, 1967), p. 26; Busia, *The Position of the Chief in the Modern Political System of Ashanti* (London: Oxford University Press, 1951).

19. Busia, *Africa in Search of Democracy*, p. 23.

20. Antubam, *Ghana's Heritage of Culture*, pp. 93 ff.; J. B. Christensen, "The Role of Proverbs in Fante Culture" in *Peoples and Cultures of Africa*, ed. E. P. Skinner (Garden City, N.Y.: Doubleday, 1973), pp. 572-73.

21. There are two types of *Ɔkyeame:* (a) *Ahenkyeame*, who is also a chief, and that is hereditary; (b) a common linguist who is appointed by the Chief because he was judged to be responsible and reliable and was generally capable of fulfilling the roles of an *Ɔkyeame*.

22. According to the beliefs of Akan society, there is a necessity for a hierarchy of power in rank. A saying and a symbol forcefully make this point. The saying is *Dibere nyinaa nnsɛ; bi da bi akyir*—i.e., all ranks are not equal; they vary in importance. Some are more important than others. The symbol is the double state umbrella called *Bidabiakyir*, literally, one will be behind another.

23. It is interesting that the Methodist Church of Ghana has used *Osagyefo* of God in their lyrics. See S. G. Williamson, "The Lyrics in the Fanti Methodist Church," in *Africa*, April 1958, p. 128.

Chapter VI

1. Charles Journet, *The Meaning of Evil* (London: G. Chapman, 1963), p. 28.

2. J. S. Pobee, "Aspects of African Traditional Religion" in *Sociological Analysis*, Vol. 37, No. 1, pp. 12-13.

3. K. G. Davies, *The Royal African Company* (London: Atheneum, 1957), p. 287.

4. T. Thompson, *An Account of Two Missionary Journeys* (London: S.P.C.K., 1937), p. 688.

5. Cf. F. B. Welbourn, "Some Problems of African Christianity: Guilt and Shame" in *Christianity in Tropical Africa*, ed. C. G. Baeta (London: International African Institute and Oxford University Press, 1968), pp. 182-99.

6. Cf. E. R. Dodds, *The Greeks and the Irrational* (University of California Press, 1951), pp. 17-18.

7. Christaller, *Dictionary*, p. 513.

8. The Găs, another ethnic group from Ghana in and around Ghana's capital, Accra, have the parallel concept of *gbesi*, i.e., inward voice, bad or good.

9. I have elsewhere warned that this may not be confused with a deistic *deus remotus* or with a *deus otiosus*. See my *Aspects of African Traditional Religion*, p. 6.

10. E. Meyerowitz, "The Concept of the Soul among the Akan" in *Africa*, 1954, p. 24. See also Elizabeth Amoah, *Moral and Social Significance of Proverbs Among the Wassaws—An Akan People* (M. A. Thesis at the University of Ghana, 1974).

11. Some would go further than this to suggest that atheism goes hand in hand with evil, promotes the decay of the family, the rise of juvenile delinquency, juvenile prostitution, and so on. I am unable to go that far because many atheists are men with moral fiber.

12. D. Bonhoeffer, *Letters and Papers from Prison* (London: Fontana, 1959), p. 125.

13. E. Lohmeyer, *The Lord's Prayer* (London: Collins, 1965), p. 171.

14. Truthfulness is central to Akan society, despite the early Christian missionary castigation of Fantes as liars. At the naming ceremony, the child is exhorted to truthfulness. See my "Aspects of African Traditional Religion," p. 14.

15. W. Michaelis, Article παραπτωμα in *T.D.N.T.*, Vol. VI, p. 172. We might compare this word with the Islamic idea of *Jahiliyyah*, i.e., time of ignorance.

16. O. Michel, *Romerbrief* (Göttingen: Ruprecht, 1963), p. 106; F. J. Leenhardt, *The Epistle to the Romans* (London: Lutterworth, 1961), p. 106; C. K. Barrett, *The Epistle to the Romans* (London: A. & C. Black, 1957), p. 95.

17. Commentators are divided as to whether law in this context refers to the moral law or the ceremonial law. For example, J. Bligh, in *Galatians* (London: St. Paul Publication, 1969), pp. 292-93 refers to the ceremonial law, the positive ritual legislation concerning sacrifices, forbidden foods, etc. In this connection, the Golden Calf (Exodus 34) illustrates the sin of idolatry. However, the debate need not affect the argument here.

18. J. Héring, *The First Epistle of St. Paul to the Corinthians* (London: Epworth, 1962), p. 41; A. Robertson and A. Plummer, *I Corinthians*, I.C.C. (Edinburgh: T. & T. Clark, 1958), pp. 115-16; C. K. Barrett, *The First Epistle to the Corinthians* (London: A. & C. Black, 1968), p. 138.

19. H. W. Montefiore, *The Epistle to the Hebrews* (London: A. & C. Black, 1964), p. 52.

20. B. F. Westcott, *The Epistles of John* (London: Macmillan, 1883), p. 99.

21. *Hamartia* has a cognate, *hamartēma*, e.g., Matt. 3:28; 4:12; Rom. 3:25; and I Cor. 6:18. It is used when sin is considered in its separate outcomings or deeds of disobedience to the divine law.

22. Christaller, *Dictionary of the Ashanti and Fante Language*. Rev. and enl. by J. Schweizer. (Basel, 1933), p. 367.

23. *Ibid.*, p. 375.

24. Akan ethics insists that morality is action. The proverb is that *abrabb ho nhomahoma no wbdze anantsenantsew tsetsew mu*—to succeed in life one must be up and doing.

25. E. H. Mends, "The Concept of Mbusu in the Ritual Ceremonies of the Fante" in *Ghana Bulletin of Theology*, Vol. 4, No. 2, pp. 14-24.

26. Leenhardt, *The Epistle to the Romans*, p. 146.

27. W. D. Davies, *Paul and Rabbinic Judaism* (London: S.P.C.K., 1955), pp. 54-57; H. Strack and P. Billerbeck, *Kommentar zum neuen Testament* (Munich, 1922), III, 222; G. F. Moore, *Judaism* (Cambridge: Harvard University Press,

1962), p. 476; N. P. Williams, *The Ideas of the Fall and of Original Sin* (London: S.P.C.K., 1927).

28. H. Schlier, *Principalities and Powers in the New Testament* (London: Herder, 1961), pp. 18-19.

29. Rom. 7:18-19; Ovid, *Metamorphoses* vii. 20f; Epictetus II. xxvi. 4.

30. There is another possible translation: I bear my Creator no grudge but my lazy parents who turned me into a beggar and expected me to feed them.

31. We do not assume the entire philosophical apparatus of St. Anselm. Basic to his argument are three philosophical principles: possibility (Latin, *potestas* = *potentia*), necessity and contingency (Latin, *voluntas*). What is necessary is to show a belief to be reasonable, so as to challenge unbelievers to produce reasons contrary and ruinous to one's own. Necessity is what can be supported by human reasons so good that no better can be alleged against them. Possibility means that which as far as we can see is most becoming. See also Anselm, *Cur Deus Homo?* See also G. Every, *Lamb for the Slaughter* (James Clarke, 1957).

32. J. B. Danquah, *Akan Doctrine of God*, p. ix.

33. In Akan society, continued sin destroys the perpetrator's personality. He says *Mogya mpa ɔtɛn tirim da*—there is always blood in the head of a tsetsefly. A wicked man is always prone to evil.

Chapter VII

1. The figures for the 1970 Census had not been released at the time of this writing. But it is not anticipated that there will be any drastic changes.

2. Marriage Ordinance, November 1844. Mohammedan Marriage Ordinance, 1907.

3. C. Hulsen and Fr. Mertens, *Survey of the Church in Ghana* (Accra: Pro Mundi Vita), chapter 8, "Marriage and the Family," p. 15.

4. The word "concubine" is often misused. Technically it refers to a woman who is living with a man, has a recognized position, but is not legally the wife. As practiced in Africa, the concubine's recognized position comes from the man having gone through certain stipulated motions under custom. It is a sort of halfway house to marriage. But she must be distinguished from the paramour who has an *ad hoc* relationship with the man and is not officially countenanced by the girl's relatives.

5. *Golden Shore*, April 1939, p. 413.

6. *White Paper on Marriage, Divorce and Inheritance*, White Paper No. 3/61 (Accra, 1961).

7. See chapter 3.

8. The Rt. Rev. M. S. O'Rorke, *Life and Work in the Diocese of Accra During 1922. Report to S.P.G.* (1922).

9. The involvement of the fellowship of believers and God has its counterpart in traditional society where all members of the clan are expected to be there with or without invitation. Traditional society also involves the ancestral spirits by libation. Of course, the ancestors are considered to be part of the clan.

10. Not all denominations regard matrimony as a sacrament. But that need not affect the argument here. Our evidence for the objectivity of the sacrament is (a) the eighth canon of the Council of Arles, A.D. 314; (b) Council of Nicaea, A.D. 325; (c) Augustine, *De Baptismo* iv. 18.

11. V. von Rad, *Old Testament Theology* (Edinburgh: Oliver and Boyd, 1962), p. 150. I am not quite happy with the expression "one flesh"; I would prefer an expression such as "a unit" or "a unity."

12. Kethuboth vii. 10.

13. H. L. Strack and P. Billerbeck, *Kommentar zum Neuen Testament aus Talmud und Midrasch* (Munich, 1923), I, 312.
14. "Marriage, Family and Household" in *A Study of Contemporary Ghana* ed. W. Birmingham, I. Neustadt and E. N. Omaboe (Evanston: Northwestern University Press, 1966).
15. *Book of Common Prayer*, Preface to Holy Matrimony.
16. Literally: if you do demand that your mother pay her debt to you, you will go to meet your father's debts.
17. It is bad enough for a woman to be infertile; but it is worse still for the man, more so partly because procreation is an absolute necessity in man's world. The Akan expressions for such a man are significant: (a) *onnyi hɔ*—he is not there, he is nonexistent; (b) *Oawu*—he is dead. In other words, without fertility a man is dead because he leaves behind no progeny to carry on the family.
18. This may not be true of traditional African homes where the elders are obliged to discipline children, whether their own or not.
19. More often than not, the polygamy and polygyny are used interchangeably. Strictly speaking, polygamy is plural marriage involving more than one spouse simultaneously. It covers polyandry, polygyny, and cenogamy. Polygyny is a common form of polygamy in which a husband has more than one wife at the same time. Cenogamy is a form of marriage in which two or more men are married to two or more women. Polyandry is a marriage in which one woman may be married to several men at the same time. Polyandry and cenogamy do not occur in West Africa. So even if we use polygamous in this context, we are thinking of polygyny.

    Polygamous relationships have not been the preserve of Africans. In Nazi Germany the Lebensborn organization of the S.S. selected Aryan males for unmarried women and made propaganda for a system of auxiliary wives for racially pure men.
20. This has a variant: *wo yerenom anum a, wo tekrema anum*—if you have five wives, you have five tongues. Polygyny makes a man deceitful and stretches a man, possibly beyond his normal human capacity.
21. *Lambeth Conference, 1888 Report* (London: S.P.C.K., 1929).
22. I am not sure that it is right to describe this as a "witting sin." It is debatable whether polygamy is a sin or a cultural ethos.
23. The Lambeth Conference of 1888 advised that a baptised convert who took a second wife be excommunicated.
24. See E. Durkheim's theory on division of labor and mechanical solidarity in *Division of Labor in Society* (Glencoe: The Free Press, 1949).

Chapter VIII

1. A. A. Afrifa, *The Ghana Coup, 24th February 1966* (London: Frank Cass, 1966); A. A. Ocran, *A Myth is Broken* (Accra: Longmans, 1968); G. Bing, *Reap the Whirlwind* (London: MacGibbon and Kee, 1968).
2. K. A. Busia, "The Ashanti" in D. Forde, ed., *African Worlds* (London: Oxford University Press, 1954), p. 200; Busia, *The Position of the Chief in the Modern Political System of Ashanti* (London: Cass, 1968), chapter 1.
3. J. A. Annobil, *Mbebusem Nkyerekyeremu* (Cape Coast: Methodist Book Depot, 1955), pp. 51-52.
4. See also Busia, *Africa in Search of Democracy* (London: Routledge & Kegan Paul, 1967).
5. Busia, "The Ashanti," p. 200.
6. In modern times it has often been assumed that Marxism is more attractive to African societies because of the alleged natural inclination to authoritarianism.

The founding of the chief's power on God is one of the points at which traditional African society and Marxist socialism part company. Marxist socialism has for its ideal the destruction of religion, which traditional African society upholds. Second, the two disagree on the Marxist commitment to the destruction of hierarchy, which in the view of the Akan is essential to the good society. Even if the two seem to agree on the theme of the equality of man, traditional society seeks it in the highest sphere of human existence, i.e., in relation to God and the ancestors; Marxism, on the other hand, seeks that goal by destroying all the higher aspects of the personality, i.e., private property, the family. In our view, traditional African society is nearer the truth because a fundamental characteristic of human society is the existence of individual relations between people. Relationships arise in which one member plays an irreplaceable role in the life of another. Besides, the basic human forces which promote the development of individuality are religion, morality, the feeling of personal participation in history, a sense of responsibility for the fate of mankind.

7. J. S. Pobee, "Church and State in the New Testament" in the *Legon Journal of the Humanities*, Vol. 1, No. 1, pp. 104-15; J. S. Pobee, "Christian Responsibility in State and Society" in *God's Mission in Ghana*, ed. W. Brandful (Accra: Asempa Press, 1974), pp. 67-68.

8. J. Macdonald, *The Theology of the Samaritans* (London: S.C.M., 1964), pp. 11-28.

9. Thomas Aquinas, *Summa Theologica* II. 2. 14 qu. 11 art. 3 (Trans. J. C. Dawson in A.P. d'Entrèves, *Aquinas Selected Political Writings*)

10. This is a much more involved issue than we appear to make it out. For feelings of love and humility are quite powerless against the power exercised by language and symbols in the creation of society, if the Christian or church resorts to exclusivist language and symbols. Such language leads to certain social sentiments and customs, as well as structures.

11. Howard Zin, "The Force of Non-violence" in *The Nation*, March 17, 1962, p. 229.

Index